NEW QUILTS FROM AN OLD

NINE×PATCH

EDITED BY **LINDA BAXTER LASCO**

AQS Publishing

Thank You, Sponsors

JANOME

Located in Paducah, Kentucky, the American Quilter's Society (AQS) is dedicated to promoting the accomplishments of today's quilters. Through its publications and events, AQS strives to honor today's quiltmakers and their work and to inspire future creativity and innovation in quiltmaking.

Executive Editor: Kimberly H. Tetrev
Senior Editor: Linda Baxter Lasco
Copy Editor: Chrystal Abhalter
Proofreader: Adriana Fitch
Graphic Design: Lynda Smith
Cover Design: Michael Buckingham
Quilt Photography: Charles R. Lynch

Additional copies of this book may be ordered from the American Quilter's Society, PO

Box 3290, Paducah, KY 42002-3290, or online at www.AmericanQuilter.com.
Text © 2015, American Quilter's Society
Artwork © 2015, American Quilter's Society

American Quilter's Society
P.O. Box 3290 • Paducah, KY 42002-3290
Fax 270-898-1173 • e-mail: orders@AQSquilt.com

Library of Congress Cataloging-in-Publication Data

Nine patch : new quilts from an old favorite / edited by Linda Baxter Lasco.
    pages cm
Includes bibliographical references and index.
ISBN 978-1-60460-180-0 (alk. paper)
1. Patchwork--Patterns. 2. Patchwork quilts--Patterns. I. Lasco, Linda Baxter, editor.
TT835.N555 2015
746.46--dc23
                    2015007127

Dedication

This book is dedicated to all those who see a traditional quilt and visualize both its link to the past and its bridge to the future.

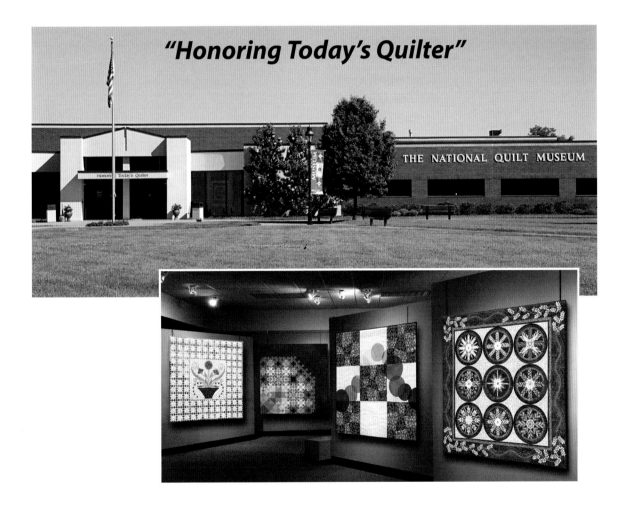

"Honoring Today's Quilter"

THE NATIONAL QUILT MUSEUM

The National Quilt Museum (NQM) is an exciting place where the public can learn more about quilts, quiltmaking, quiltmakers, and experience quilts that inspire and delight.

The museum celebrates today's quilts and quiltmakers through exhibits of quilts from the museum's collection and selected temporary exhibits. By providing a variety of workshops and other programs, The National Quilt Museum helps to encourage, inspire, and enhance the development of today's quilter.

Whether presenting new or antique quilts, the museum promotes understanding of and respect for all quilts—contemporary and antique, classical and innovative, machine made and handmade, utility and art.

Contents

Preface

While preservation of the past is one of The National Quilt Museum's core functions, one of its greatest services is performed as it links the past to the present and to the future. With that goal in mind, The National Quilt Museum sponsors an annual contest and exhibit—New Quilts from an Old Favorite (NQOF).

Created both to acknowledge our quiltmaking heritage and to recognize innovation, creativity, and excellence, the contest challenges today's quiltmakers to interpret a single traditional quilt block in a new and exciting work of their own design. Each year contestants respond with a myriad of stunning interpretations, and this year is no different.

Nine Patch: New Quilts from an Old Favorite is a collection of these interpretations. In this book, you'll find a brief description of the contest, followed by the five award winners and thirteen additional finalists and their quilts.

Full-color photographs of the quilts accompany each quiltmaker's comments—comments that provide insight into their widely diverse creative processes. The winners' and finalists' tips and techniques offer an artistic framework for your own interpretation. In addition, some information about The National Quilt Museum is included.

Our wish is that Nine Patch: New Quilts from an Old Favorite will further our quiltmaking heritage as new quilts based on this traditional block are inspired by the outstanding quilts contained within.

The Contest

The role of a museum is not only to preserve the past, but also to link the past to the present and to the future. With that goal at heart, The National Quilt Museum holds an annual contest and exhibit, New Quilts from an Old Favorite. Created to acknowledge our quiltmaking heritage and to recognize innovation, creativity, and excellence, the contest challenges today's quiltmakers to interpret a single traditional quilt block in a work of their own design.

The contest requires that quilts entered be recognizable in some way as a variation on that year's selected block. The quilts must be no larger than 80" and no smaller than 50" on a side. Each quilt entered must be quilted. Quilts may only be entered by the maker(s) and must have been completed after December 31 two years prior to the entry date.

Quiltmakers are asked to send in two images—one of the full quilt and one detail—for jurying. Three jurors view these and consider technique, artistry, and interpretation of the theme block to select 18 finalists. These finalist quilts are sent to the museum where a panel of three judges carefully evaluates them. This evaluation of the actual quilts focuses on design, innovation, theme, and workmanship. The first- through fifth-place winners are then selected and notified.

An exhibit of the 18 quilts opens at The National Quilt Museum in Paducah, Kentucky, each spring, then travels to venues around the country for two years. Thousands of quilt lovers have enjoyed these exhibits at their local or regional museums.

A book is produced by the American Quilter's Society featuring full-color photos of all the finalists and quilts, biographical information about each quilter, and their tips and techniques. The book provides an inside look at how quilts are created and a glimpse into the artistic mindset of today's quilters.

Previous theme blocks have been Double Wedding Ring, Log Cabin, Kaleidoscope, Mariner's Compass, Ohio Star, Pineapple, Storm at Sea, Bear's Paw, Tumbling Blocks, Feathered Star, Monkey Wrench, Seven Sisters, Dresden Plate, Sawtooth, Sunflower, Orange Peel, Baskets, Jacob's Ladder, and Carolina Lily. The block selected for 2015 was Nine Patch. The 2016 block will be New York Beauty. Flying Geese and Bow Tie will be the featured blocks for 2017 and 2018, respectively.

NQM would like to thank this year's New Quilts from an Old Favorite contest sponsors: Janome and MODA Fabrics.

The Nine Patch Block

The arrangement of patches that quilters know as Nine Patch is so basic to design in general, it is difficult to make statements regarding its earliest appearance and era of its highest popularity.

The simplest design unit (or quilt block) is a single square:

The next simplest design unit (or quilt block) would be a Four Patch:

The next most simple design unit would be a Nine Patch:

With each of these configurations there is corresponding increase in the possibilities for the overall design of a quilt and/or quilt block. Consider:

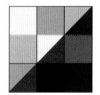

Nine Patch block elements are found in early Medallion style quilts, which were popular in the eighteenth and early nineteenth centuries. By the mid-nineteenth century, pieced block-style quilts had become the predominant design form and remain popular to this day. A block as versatile as the Nine Patch is as familiar to today's quiltmaker as it was to quiltmakers of the past.

A search for Nine Patch on The Quilt Index (www.quiltindex.org) resulted in 1,269 quilts. The breakdown of these quilts by date range reflects the growth and dominance of this simple pieced block-style quilt and generally coincides with the emerging dominance of pieced block-style quilts:

Date Range	Quilts	#Years in Range
Pre-1799	4	n/a
1800 – 1849	70	50
1850 – 1875	134	25
1876 – 1900	360	25
1901 – 1929	360	29
1930 – 1949	341	19

Names other than "Nine Patch" associated with these quilts from The Quilt Index are Framed Nine Patch, Unequal Nine Patch, Extended Nine Patch, Uneven Nine Patch, Nine Patch and Snowball, Cross Roads to Jericho, Crosses, Four Square, Single Irish Chain, Puss in the Corner, and Shoofly. In the Encyclopedia of Pieced Quilt Patterns by Barbara Brackman, there are 14 named patterns with "Nine Patch" in the title. The earliest two Nine Patch patterns were published in 1895 and 1896 and may have been published as early as 1889. These two patterns were published under eight other names as well. Many other Nine Patch-type patterns were published in the 1930s, the heyday of pattern publishing. Thus it appears that the name of this simple pattern was prettied up for marketing purposes. How else are you going to sell such a basic design?

Also noteworthy is that 22 Nine Patch doll quilts were found in The Quilt Index search. As a tool for teaching girls necessary sewing skills, the Nine Patch block would be indispensable. The repetition of cutting squares encouraged precision and the piecing stitch would have been good practice. Doll quilts generally don't last. A search on The Quilt Index using "doll quilt" and "1600 – 1949" yielded 81 quilts. That 22 of these quilts were Nine Patch quilts speaks to how sewing was taught to girls in the past. As a building block of quilt history, the importance of the Nine Patch is assured.

Judy Schwender
Curator of Collections/Registrar
The National Quilt Museum

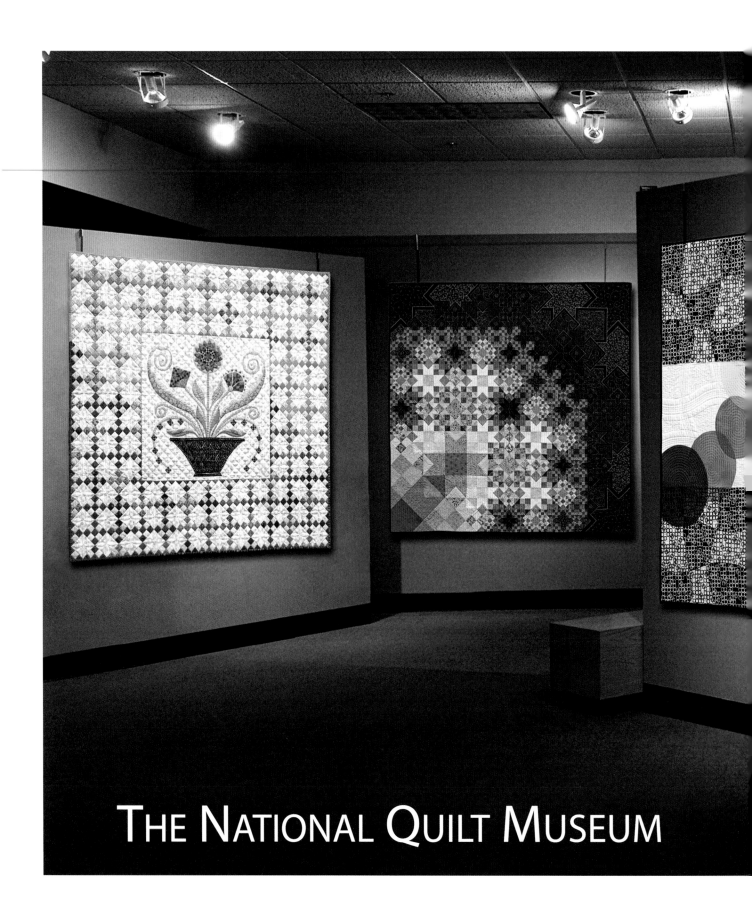

THE NATIONAL QUILT MUSEUM

First Place
Robin Gausebeck

Rockford, Illinois

Meet Robin

Ten years ago, I made my first quilt so that a blank wall in my stairwell would be filled with color. Little did I know how my world would expand over the intervening years.

Raising a family and working in accounting and finance for most of my adult life left little room for developing hobbies that required time, study, money, and a space to work. My off-hours were likely spent reading, cooking, and running. Sewing was something I did when clothes needed hemming or windows needed spruced-up curtains. Quilting was barely on my radar.

Something about the process of making that first quilt must have awakened a long-dormant artistic side and I have never regretted for a minute the time I have since spent designing, choosing fabrics, stitching, and quilting. Well, maybe once or twice when what seemed like a good idea took a rapid trip downhill.

Through quilting I have been able to nurture my creativity and love of color. I have traveled to places for the first time—attending a quilt show or retreat is always a great excuse! I have made numerous friends, some virtual and many more in the flesh. All of these experiences continue to inspire me to grow and expand my repertoire of ideas and techniques.

2014 has been a very good year in my quilting life. My quilt DANS LES BAINS DE MAROC received the A-1 Quilting Best Miniature award in Paducah and is now part of the permanent collection of The National Quilt Museum. I received my first blue ribbon at the IQA Festival in Houston and REVOLUTION #9 graces the cover of this book.

I will probably enter New Quilts from an Old Favorite through its twenty-fifth year and then maybe take a break. This contest has been loads of fun for me since my first entry with the Sawtooth block. I generally do not make traditional quilts, so the concept of taking something traditional and turning it into something contemporary appeals to me. I plan to work more improvisationally in the future and start to play around with abstract ideas and designs. Who knows where that will lead?

My greatest supporter remains my husband, Steve, who is not offended when I don't take his advice but continues to give it when asked. He has gotten to know many people in the quilting world and loves to bring friends to The National Quilt Museum where he is a knowledgeable guide for whatever is on exhibit. Best of all, he gets as excited as I do by each of my accomplishments. I couldn't ask for a better friend and spouse.

Inspiration and Design

I have always appreciated wordplay; even though I work as a quilt artist, my first inclination when designing a new quilt has been to describe in words what I want to do. I will sit and brainstorm ideas, motifs, and techniques; I usually work from a quilt title that has somehow popped into my head. What I generally don't do is sketch. That seems, even to me, a funny way for an artist to work.

REVOLUTION #9

70" x 53"

In the spring of 2013, I was lucky enough to attend one of Ricky Tims' retreats in Colorado. I had just been commissioned by the Rockford Symphony Orchestra to make a quilt for them to auction at their annual fundraiser. With Ricky's dual interests in quilting and music, this retreat seemed like the perfect venue to get this quilt underway. I began my usual process of setting down in words what I wanted to accomplish but somehow I wasn't getting any further than the title "Appassionata." Ricky immediately sensed my problem (how simple it seems to me now): "Make visual decisions visually."

Ricky had me draw small boxes in roughly the shape of the finished quilt and quickly fill them with doodles, lines, shapes—anything I could think of and sketch in literally a couple of seconds. I had several pages of them in just a short while.

Then he directed me to choose the one or two I liked best and expand them into the raw material for a quilt. All of a sudden, the ideas flowed and I had the architecture for my quilt. Designing the appliqués and other details took a while longer, but by the end of the first day of the retreat I was ready to start sewing.

I actually fell in love with the finished quilt and determined that if given a chance, I would expand the design into something more complex. The Nine Patch challenge was the perfect vehicle. I was able to expand my original idea into something larger that retained the feeling that I wanted.

Being a Beatles fan of long standing, I had my title, REVOLUTION #9, before I had my finished design. Couple that with the fact that my little granddaughter Charlotte's favorite number is 9 (Who knew kids had favorite numbers?) and this quilt nearly designed itself.

Charlotte enjoys making "quilts" in my studio and has a stable of preferred colors, so I used two of them in the quilt—pink and turquoise. One further nod to her influence is the pink dot that appears in several places. It is a play on a wonderful pop-up book titled *One Red Dot*, by David A. Carter, in which the goal is to find one red dot hidden in each of several masterful paper constructions.

Obviously, since this was a Nine Patch challenge, I had to find ways to integrate that block into a quilt whose lines were all swooping curves. There are subtle and not-so-subtle references scattered throughout the quilt: Nine Patch diamonds appear in the big wheel; small squares and circles are arranged in 3 x 3 arrays in some of the other wheels; I included implied Nine Patch blocks with black painted in all of the white ribbons; and finally I appliquéd some 9s in case it still wasn't clear what this quilt was about. This is really the heart of NQOF—finding innovative and unexpected ways to include the chosen block.

Fabric selection was by far the biggest challenge with this quilt. I made a small mockup of the design to play around with color placement, but small pieces of fabric just weren't effective in giving me an overall view of what the larger pieces would look like, particularly since I wanted to use as much ombre fabric as I could.

The ombre fabric would provide variation in the large spaces but would still give the impression that each large "swoop" was just one color. In the end, I really had to audition the various fabrics in the actual size and shape of each piece, place them on my design wall, observe, and think about them before I really knew which fabrics would work and which ones wouldn't. I would estimate that at least half the fabrics I thought would work ended up back in my stash or in my scrap bins.

Challenge number two was designing the quilting. I normally have a rough idea of how I want the quilting to look and then just sit down at the machine and improvise. For this quilt, I tried something completely new for me. I actually planned the quilting out beforehand and marked the entire top. This was truly a game-changer. It forced me to think more mindfully about what I was trying to communicate with the quilting. Were there ways to thematically tie the quilting into the Nine Patch idea? What sources of inspiration could I turn to? Traditional henna designs from India provided some particularly good ideas. I know this all seems very basic to most quilters but I had never before been as mindful of the quilting part of the design process. Perhaps it was the need to fill large spaces that forced me to think in a new way. In any case, I know that I will never again approach the quilt design process without paying careful attention to the quilting.

Binding Technique

Many people who have seen this quilt have remarked on the embroidered binding. This is a technique I have wanted to explore ever since I first saw Marla Yeager's quilt BUCKSKIN, that hangs in The National Quilt Museum. A decorative binding is one of those little details that can enhance the appeal of any quilt. It looks more difficult than it is and requires only two things—a machine that can sew at least one zigzag or decorative stitch and some patience. If your machine lacks built-in decorative stitches, you can try to customize your own zigzag stitch by varying the stitch width and length. Even a plain large zigzag might look good with an interesting variegated thread. For another twist, particularly if your quilt is a very colorful one, try changing the color of your stitching at intervals.

A couple of years ago, after a workshop with Pat Holly, I took her suggestion and made small samples of all the decorative stitches that my BERNINA® aurora 440 QE had in its memory.

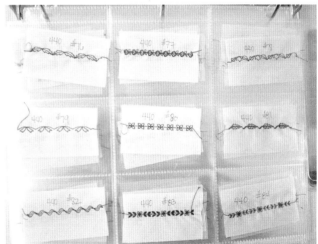

The initial step in making this binding, then, was to go through my samples and find a stitch that would look good with a nice variegated thread and be the appropriate style and size for the binding. In this instance, I chose stitch #82. After that, this is what to do:

1. Cut and piece binding strips in the usual way. For a binding that will finish at ¼", I like to cut my strips 2⅛" wide. This width seems to yield a nice, tight binding with no unfilled edges.

2. Carefully spray-starch the entire binding strip twice or three times, spraying and ironing from the back side. Be careful not to distort the binding when you iron. Let the strip dry completely between applications of the starch. This provides a stiff fabric that will fold with a nice crease and will not require any kind of stabilizer to keep the embroidery from "drawing up." I use Stay-Flo® Liquid Starch diluted 1:1 with water and apply it with a spray bottle.

3. Lay the binding on a large flat surface and determine where you think the center line of the decorative stitching should be. For my binding, the mark was ⁷⁄₁₆" from either edge. Since I started with black fabric, I marked this line with a Clover® White Marking Pen, an iron-off marker.

Any marker that shows up well on the chosen fabric will work. In most cases, the mark will either rub off in the process of stitching or be covered up by the stitching itself. NOTE: An alternative to marking the fabric strip is to tape a stack of Post-it® Notes forward and to the right of your throat plate so you can feed the strip under the needle at the required place.

4. Now here's where the patience comes in. Going moderately slowly and maintaining good control, sew the entire length of the binding strip with your chosen decorative stitch using your marked center line to keep your stitching straight.

My quilt measured 70" x 53", so the binding strip I made was approximately 272" long, allowing extra for the corners and the join. This is a good activity to do while listening to music, as it is NOT a quick process!

5. Once the entire strip has been stitched, take it back to the ironing board and press the binding in half lengthwise, wrong sides together.

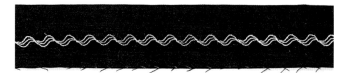

As I'm ironing, I feed my folded binding into a small paper bag with handles. This makes for easy transporting as I alternately pin and sew each side of the quilt.

6. Pin the binding to the quilt with the decorative side of the binding next to the front of the quilt. Attach the binding, mitering the corners and joining the ends as with any other binding. DON'T WORRY ABOUT WHAT THE DECORATIVE STITCH DESIGN DOES AT THE CORNER MITERS OR AT THE FINAL JOIN! If you have stitched in a relatively straight line and sewn the binding on properly, the lines of stitching will meet nicely at the corners and it doesn't matter one iota if the decorative stitching does not look like a continuous pattern.

7. Turn the binding to the back and hand stitch. The result? A unique binding that handsomely finishes your beautiful quilt.

Second Place
Jane Zillmer
Mercer, Wisconsin

Photo by Carla Fahden

Meet Jane

It seems I have always been interested in needle and thread, and I've tried and enjoyed many types of hand and machine stitching.

Growing up in a home that had quilts handmade by my mother on every bed, it seems natural that I developed an interest in quilt making. When I was in high school I designed and made my first quilt, which I still own.

My two daughters allowed me the wonderful pleasure of sewing all their clothes when they were young. Simple outfits were the perfect canvas to try out a new technique I learned at a machine appliqué class. Of course, I made them appliquéd bed quilts, too, even before I started really quilting in earnest.

Later I took my first quilting class, and the project, a quilt sampler of traditional blocks, was entirely made by hand. I then took a machine quilting class and became completely hooked on quilting.

I made bed quilts, wall quilts, warm thick woolen tied quilts, quilts for gifts—I couldn't make enough quilts!

In the midst of this frenzy, I heard about a local quilt show looking for entries. I entered one of my early "masterpieces" and won first place. The fun of sharing my quilt with others and winning a ribbon spurred me to continue entering tougher competitions, improving my work with each new quilt I made.

Of course, I love attending quilt shows, too, and am always in awe of and inspired by the work that is displayed.

To have show judges critique my quilts and write comments is an added bonus; it helps me continue to improve my work. My show quilts have won awards and with their recognition led me down the path to writing a book of my quilts titled *Nature's Journey Appliqué* (AQS 2013). I also write a blog, which spurs me to move along with my work and share with others (www.woodsandwildflowersappliquéart. blogspot.com).

I design all my own quilts and most are almost entirely appliquéd. Motifs are drawn on paper and this is one of the most enjoyable parts of the quiltmaking process for me.

Quiltmaking is a very important part of almost every day, even if it's just for a short time. I always have projects in the works at different stages, whether creating new designs, cutting, stitching, or quilting. My sewing "lab" overlooks our lake and the woods. It is very quiet and peaceful. Our two cats, Leo and Lily, often visit me there and beg me to stop and play with them.

DECEMBER is one of my favorite quilts. I have thought of making a collection of quilts for each month of the year, maybe all the same size and based on the Nine Patch block. There is something of beauty and uniqueness to find every month of the year in nature.

DECEMBER

58" x 58"

Inspiration and Design

My daily walks among the beauty of nature in northern Wisconsin often provide inspiration for my quilt designs.

I have grown to love the peace and calm of December in all its darkness. Most days are cloud-covered and gray. The only colors I see are the dark greens and browns of pine trees. However, when the clouds do lift, the blue sky is stunning. Now add the main attraction of this month—snow!

With these designs, images, and colors in mind and starting with the basic Nine Patch block, DECEMBER became a quilt.

It seems many of my quilts incorporate circles, large or small, either as a major design element or accent. Circles are easy to look at and understand and may be calming, just like the month of December. The black circle backgrounds were easily chosen to showcase my snowflakes. I then added three randomly pieced circular borders to each black circle in deep browns and greens to represent winter pine trees.

Now I had a blank canvas for my snowflake appliqués. I drew them on graph paper, starting with a circle of the same size at the center of each block. I chose to design each snowflake using botanical or outdoor motifs rather than plain graphics.

I had designed eight of the nine snowflake circles when I reached a "quilter's block" (like a writer's block) with no inspiration coming to me. That blank canvas stared at me for a long time.

My design process often takes place in my subconscious. While not actually looking for an idea, one will just come to me. One day in spring, huge icicles had formed on a warm day, dropping from roof edges and eaves. Aha! A depiction of those icicles became the center block design and my favorite.

With the Nine Patches completed and pieced, now it was time to add the borders. Studying the top pinned to my design wall, I initially thought maybe no borders were needed with such striking block designs. But as I let it hang there and gaze at me for some time, the top said to me, "Yes, borders."

But what to do? Designing the borders took many, many hours. I used Electric Quilt 7® (EQ7) software and came up with many possible pieced borders, but I decided to design appliquéd borders instead. I cut many actual motifs to audition them before finally drawing and choosing the right one—a simple sprig not found in the Snowflake blocks.

I offset the corner border appliqués to add interest and stitched the green vine around the entire quilt border, using it as the stem for my machine quilting.

Considering myself a novice at machine quilting, this became the biggest challenge when making this quilt. I know how much quilting adds to a quilt. I didn't plan my quilting designs while planning the quilt, but did so as I went along. By using a light thread in the bobbin to accent quilt all the snowflake motifs, I surprised myself at the nice design this added to the back of the quilt. Lots of extra practice and patience helped me accomplish the machine quilting.

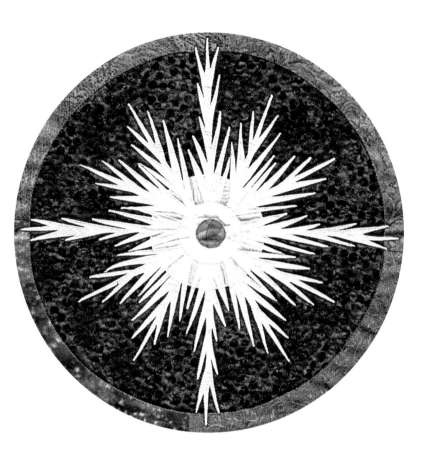

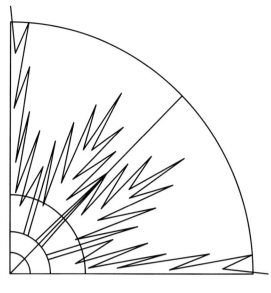

Enlarge patterns 200%

Third Place
Nancy Eisenhauer

Belleville, Illinois

Photo by Gerard Reuter

Meet Nancy

I came to quilting late, after retiring from teaching elementary students for 35 years. For me, quilting has become much more than just a pastime. It is a passion. However, I have loved fabrics and sewing for a long time. During my lifetime, fabrics, fashion, and quilting have gone through many style changes. My grandmother quilted when other chores on the farm were finished. I remember seeing her work in progress as far back as the late 1950s. Sometimes she embroidered blocks for a quilt and occasionally made matching pillowcases. She was also an appliquér. She traced shapes onto cereal boxes and cut everything with scissors. I'm pretty sure by the 60s or 70s some polyester was worked into her quilts. I remember one glorious Lone Star quilt. She usually worked with solids unless she was using scraps from dresses and aprons.

When I started sewing, I used whatever fabrics were in fashion at the time. Cotton and wool gave way to polyesters, and eventually I found my way to silk, brocade, tapestry, and back to cotton. I've enjoyed trying an assortment of techniques and styles in my quilts. I have tried piecing, paper piecing, appliqué—both hand and machine—painted canvas, beading, dyeing, discharging, and inking, among other things. It seems there is always a new technique or design concept to explore.

I have jumped from style to style. I tried watercolor quilts, embellishing with yo-yos, piecing those dark Kansas Troubles, bargello, and T-shirt quilts—all before I began constructing my own designs. I have never seemed to be able to settle on a style. I like working with basic shapes and skewing them into

something interesting. Color is very important to me. Much of my inspiration comes from artists who used color boldly. Piet Mondrian and Vincent Van Gogh are my favorites. Line also plays an important part in my designs. Anything that gives an impression of motion is appealing to me. I seem to use lots of curves.

I really like the modern quilt style. I like the clean lines and clear colors. IT'S NOT ALL BLACK AND WHITE is my first attempt at a quilt in that style. The rigid geometry of a Nine Patch block seemed to lend itself to the modern quilt style. Of course, I added some curves. I think I'll continue to explore the use of color and line in modern quilts.

Inspiration

A quilt I remember from my earliest days is a Nine Patch quilt that was on my parents' bed, made by my grandmother. There were recognizable fabrics from Grandma's scraps set with white muslin. I remember sitting on the bed and picking out fabrics I recognized from Grandma's dresses, aprons, and doll clothing. I was fascinated by the colors and patterns. It was a happy quilt with lots of color playing on that snowy background. It went to quilt heaven long ago, but it lives in my mind. It wasn't a conscious inspiration, but I know it is always in my reserve of memories and design schemes. The colors on white were the beginning of my design. I also love black-and-white prints. Combine the two and I was ready to go.

The simple graphics of the Nine Patch block seemed to lead me to the modern quilt style. What can you do with the simple crosshatch that looks like a tic-tac-toe grid? I explored skewing the design in

IT'S NOT ALL BLACK AND WHITE

54" x 54"

an assortment of ways. How about making the squares into diamonds? How about combining scales and making a Nine Patch within a Nine Patch? How about a circular Nine Patch? (I couldn't make that work at all!) How about a curvy Nine Patch?

My favorite design tool is a notebook of quarter-inch grid paper. Add a pencil and a ruler and I'm ready. For me it is easy to start with an idea, get something on paper, and flip to the next page to start again as needed. (Did I tell you how I love my Pink Pearl® eraser?) Sometimes I wind up going back to an early design for a rework. I also like the grid paper because it is so easy to blow up the design by increasing the size of the grid squares. Low tech? Very, but it suits the way I like to work.

Because of the size of the grid, I can easily hand-draw small curves that will become large sweeping curves on the finished quilt. That is where I started once I had blocked off the large Nine Patch on paper. I drew the curved grids in the four corners and center block, where I intended to use black-and-white fabrics. The curved grids in the all-white blocks happened later when I was ready to quilt.

Next, I wanted to add color. I love transparency techniques and have used them before in quilts. A rainbow of circles seemed to fit with the curvy blocks. I used several sizes of circles and curved them across the quilt. The trick was going to be how to make the circles look like transparent-colored circles laid on top of both the printed and solid fabrics. That was a problem to be solved later. For now I had a design with which I was happy.

Techniques

This quilt was fairly simple to execute, with one exception: how to get those

colored circles to look transparent on both the white solid fabric and the prints. I love the look of transparent fabrics and have done some quilts using

transparency, but always with commercial fabrics. For this project I needed a way to color white fabric and two black-and-white prints that were a different brand from the plain white. I have used painted fabric in some other quilts, so I knew that painting the fabric would definitely change the hand.

I tried a couple of brands of paint that I had at home on each of the fabrics. One was definitely brighter than the other. One brand was eliminated.

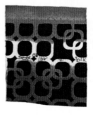 

As I tried various colors of the preferred paint, I found that the lighter colors, especially yellow, covered the black portions of the black-and-white print too well. By painting from the back of the fabric, I improved the look. I liked the look of the fabric as I tried a range of colors, from light to dark.

The remaining problem was the stiffness of the fabric once painted. A friend had been using inks to color fabric and was pleased with the results. I tried some of her spray inks intended for use on paper for scrapbooking. It worked well. I found that I could control the saturation of color by dampening or not dampening the fabric before I applied the ink. The colors mixed well, both as they were sprayed on or mixed in a small container and applied with a brush. I tried the inks on the white and black-and-white prints, and found that the color was taken exactly the same way on both types of fabric. Good news!

Fortunately, I had bought plenty of fabric. I experimented with getting the shade and depth of color just as I wanted it. I was able, for example, to get a more saturated yellow for the area where two yellow disks overlapped. Not all of the colors of ink behaved the same way when applied to fabric; so as I found the color I wanted, I inked the pieces I needed for the quilt. Careful labeling was essential. I felt like a mad scientist playing in my lab. It was a lot of fun!

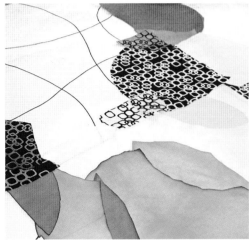

When it was time to assemble all these strangely shaped pieces in a variety of sizes, I used Katie Pasquini-Masopust's construction technique for her art quilts. By pressing under some edges and overlapping them onto unturned adjoining edges, I got the clean, smooth look I wanted. I had a full-sized pattern on which I placed the pieces for each block. By carefully placing the pieces, I was able to sew the blocks together and get the continuous look I was after.

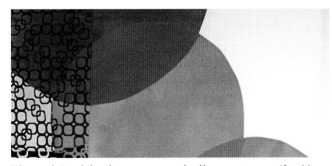

The white blocks were a challenge to quilt. How much quilting was too much? Do I make the design of those blocks continuous with the print blocks, or do they stand alone? White thread or black? In the end I chose to continue the serpentine lines of the other blocks in the quilting, but do it in white rayon thread

so there would be a lot of contrast between the white and print blocks. I'm happy with the results.

Fourth Place
Amy Krasnansky

Baltimore, Maryland

Photo by Alyssa Krasnansky

Meet Amy

I became addicted to quilting 14 years ago when I made a baby quilt for my nephew. It was composed of Log Cabin blocks in yellows and greens. I arranged the blocks to look like a leaf. The whole process was a wonderful experience. I finally found the true purpose of a fabric store while picking the palette of fabrics for the quilt. I loved how quickly the blocks came together with chain piecing. Also, combining the finished blocks and seeing the end result was so satisfying.

So, I scoured the Baltimore County library system for pretty much every book about quilting that they had. (I was addicted to reading long before I acquired the quilting habit.) I practiced lots of techniques on quilts for family and friends. I still can't settle on one technique, and I learn more with every quilt I make.

Now I have gotten to the point where I make quilts not just to give as gifts or because I have some wall space or bed space to fill, but as self-expression. This means that I have piles of self-expression all over my house with no place to put them. I recently created a website (seamslikerain.weebly.com) with a blog and an Etsy store in the hopes of sharing my quilts with the world and possibly selling a few.

Since I began viewing quiltmaking from an artistic standpoint, my perception of the world around me has sharpened. Now I notice the shape the tree branches make against the sky, the progression of colors in a sunset, and the way the raindrops on the windshield contain the taillights of the cars in front of me. So many beautiful and interesting things surround us; being able

to focus on them seems to be a blessing that comes from practicing art.

I live in Baltimore with my husband and two children. And no, I haven't made a Baltimore Album quilt. When I am not quilting, I work part-time as a software engineer, serve at my church, tend my garden, read voraciously, and attempt to ignore the dust bunnies hiding in the corners of my house.

Inspiration and Design

I like to play with scale and I have been interested in fractals for several years. A fractal is a pattern that repeats at every scale so that what you see if you zoom in is the same or similar to what you see if you zoom out. Trees are a classic example from nature— branches separating into branches that separate into more branches until you are down to the smallest twigs.

Since the Nine Patch block is simple, it seemed like a good candidate for experiments in fractals. The most obvious way to do a fractal Nine Patch would be to put a smaller Nine Patch in one or more of the squares of a larger Nine Patch, and then put an even smaller Nine Patch in the small Nine Patch, and so on. Since each successive level is one-ninth the size of the previous level, it quickly becomes impossible to construct.

FRACTAL BLOOMS

61" x 61"

I was hoping to come up with something less static and square, something with more movement and interest. So, I thought about tree branches. I drew Nine Patch blocks branching off from each side of the original block on the diagonal.

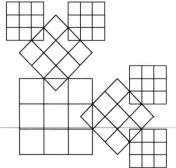

Now each successive branch was about two-thirds the size of the previous one, allowing me more iterations before it became too small to construct.

I wanted each iteration to be unified in some way and to lead into the next iteration. I also needed to be able to distinguish the squares on the Nine Patch. I considered using reproduction fabrics and moving from Civil War fabrics in the largest block through various fabric eras in the mid-sized blocks to contemporary fabrics in the smallest blocks. This is one of the fabric combinations I produced in EQ7 for this idea. Perhaps, dear reader, you can see why I abandoned the concept.

In the end, I decided to use value to create the Nine Patch—alternating light and dark in a checkerboard pattern—and hue to distinguish the different-size iterations. I started with blue on the biggest block and moved through green, yellow, orange, red, and magenta, ending with purple on the smallest blocks.

Where the blocks overlapped, I chose colors carefully to give the illusion that the smaller block was translucent. I drew the quilt in a drawing program (GIMP/Gnu Image Manipulation Program) on my computer. This allowed me to put each block size in its own layer and adjust the transparency level of each layer to give the look that I wanted. Then I used the colors on the drawing as a guide for selecting fabrics.

For the quilting, I used the same fractal design with squares instead of Nine Patch blocks. I left a border without quilting around the edge of each square so that the black fabric would outline the square. I chose threads that matched the colors I had selected for the blocks. Then I browsed Leah Day's Free Motion Quilting Project website (http://freemotionquilting.blogspot.com/p/365-designs.html) for ideas for quilting patterns. I wanted a different pattern for each size square. I ended up with flowers for the pink and purple squares, and various freeform designs for the others. When I looked at it after finishing the quilting, I felt that the fractal pattern was not as visible as I wanted it to be, so I outlined each square by hand with a stem stitch using embroidery floss.

Technique

To give the illusion that a translucent shape is overlapping another shape, there are four fabrics to consider: the bottom shape, the top shape, the overlap piece, and the background fabric.

This figure shows a blue rectangle and a red rectangle both at fifty-percent opacity over a white background. The blue rectangle is on top.

Here are the same rectangles with the red rectangle on top. Notice that the overlapped area is a bluer purple when the blue is on top and a redder purple when the red is on top.

In both cases, the overlap is darker than the red and the blue because less of the white background is showing through where the colors overlap. So, if you wanted to create the illusion of translucency on a light background, you would pick a fabric for the overlapped area that is darker than your two overlapping fabrics, mixes the two colors, and leans toward the color of the shape you want to appear on top.

This figure shows what the rectangles shown in the previous figure look like on a black background. The rectangles are darker than they were on the light background, of course, because the black is showing through. The overlap is lighter than both of the rectangles because less of the black is showing through in that area.

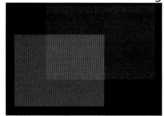

If you wanted to create the illusion of translucency on a dark background, you would pick a fabric for the overlap that is lighter than either of the two overlapping fabrics. Of course, you are not limited to white and black backgrounds. The easiest way to see the colors that result is to use a drawing program that allows layers. Draw colored rectangles in separate layers from the background and change the layer opacity on the rectangle layers to fifty percent (or whatever you like). Then play with the colors of the background and the rectangles and see what happens.

Generally, the illusion of translucency is only going to hold if you use fabrics that read as a single color from a distance, so you should only use solids or tone-on-tone fabrics or small-scale print fabrics.

However, sometimes a fabric collection contains the same print with two different background colors. Then you can create the illusion that the print is floating over two different solids.

The two solid colors need to have corresponding relationships with the two print backgrounds. In this case, the blue and green solids are each a couple of steps darker than the print backgrounds. I could have chosen to make them both lighter. However, if I matched the print backgrounds, the print would

blend in and lose its square shape. Although that could be the intended effect, usually some contrast is desirable to delineate the shape.

The scale of the print should allow the print background to be clearly visible. For example, if the design calls for 3" squares, it would not work well with a print with lots of 4" flowers.

When using a large-scale or high-contrast print, the pattern will have to match at the seams. This is easier than it sounds, although you will need to buy extra fabric. Lay the two fabrics out so that the print goes in the same direction for each one. Then start overlapping until you have lined up the pattern. Once you see where they line up, trim that edge on the top fabric, fold it under to make a ½" seam allowance. and iron it down. Then put it back on top of the other fabric, lining up the pattern again. Lift the edge a little at a time and put a light bead of temporary fabric glue on the seam allowance to hold it in place, adjusting it so that the pattern lines up when you put the edge down. Once the glue is dry, sew inside the crease of the top fabric. Then you can trim the seam allowances to ¼".

Fifth Place
Tere D'Amato

Mashpee, Massachusetts

Meet Tere

My father, a military officer with six children, believed that a growing child's wardrobe needed no more than a school uniform, a church outfit, and play clothes. Fortunately for me, he saw sewing as a practical skill his daughters should master. There were no restrictions on materials needed for "sewing lessons." Before I graduated from high school, my mother, an excellent seamstress, taught me to sew a prom dress, tailor a suit, slipcover a chair, and knit a sweater. My parents sent me to college with two valuable gifts—a string of pearls and an Elna Supermatic.

Sewing continued to give me years of pleasure. When my future husband asked me to marry him, he jokingly said, "I don't know whether to buy you a diamond ring or a new sewing machine." I missed the irony and soon was the proud owner of a sewing machine that embroidered. Even now, I wear a simple gold band but sew on a top of the line sewing machine.

While attending a machine embroidery class, I popped into the next classroom to see what the quilters were doing. With flannel design walls hung around the room, I was surrounded by dizzying color. The following day I switched to the quilting class and was hooked. The resulting quilt, KYOTO CIRCLES, remains one of my favorites.

After that first class, I immersed myself in quilting. New England is fortunate to attract the country's best teachers—not only do we have wonderful quilt shops, but quilt conferences bring us vendors from all over the country. Soon even my vacations were spent traveling to events like the AQS shows. I now have enough notions, thread, and fat quarters to open a small quilt shop! Quilting is not just my hobby; it is an obsession.

FRESH FROM MY NINE PATCH GARDEN is my first entry in a quilt competition. Even before I was notified that my quilt was a finalist, I knew it would not be my last. The day I shipped my entry form off to The National Quilt Museum, my husband and I took the train into New York City. I came back with the inspiration for the New York Beauty block, the 2016 contest theme.

What have I learned from entering my first quilt contest? First, set your personal deadline well before the contest deadline. Let your ideas marinate before committing to a design—test and test again. Stay flexible and leave plenty of time to rip out and redo.

Second, don't assume your skills are not good enough to compete nationally. FRESH FROM MY NINE PATCH GARDEN was my best work, but I wondered if it was good enough. Then my friends reminded me that a best-in-show winner in one contest may not win a ribbon in the next.

Lastly, if you enter a contest in Paducah and hope to see your quilt hanging there, book your room when you mail off your entry, just in case!

FRESH FROM
MY NINE PATCH GARDEN

50" x 50"

Inspiration and Design

A visit to The National Quilt Museum during AQS QuiltWeek® – Paducah 2014 sparked my imagination. I couldn't get the Nine Patch block out of my mind after learning it was the theme of the 2015 contest. Flying home from Paducah, I dozed off thinking about the popular Blooming Nine Patch quilt pattern and woke up envisioning Nine Patch blooms. By the time I landed in Boston, the margins of my airline magazine were filled with sketches. I couldn't wait to get to a sketchpad and colored pencils.

The final design of this quilt reflects my love of whimsy, color, and a technical challenge. Its whimsical nature was inspired by the work of Becky Goldsmith and Linda Jenkins of Piece O' Cake designs. I kept their aesthetic in mind as I sketched. As I am not a trained artist, I relied on graph paper, plastic appliqué templates, a set of French curve rules from the local art supply store, and a very large eraser.

The colors for the quilt were inspired by a double-split complement fabric print by Anna Marie Horner. A double-split complement combination is created by identifying a primary color and its complement (such as red and green), then using the colors to the right and left of those colors on the color wheel (yellow-green, blue-green, red-violet, and red-orange). By varying the values between medium-light, medium, and medium-dark choices, a balanced quilt design resulted.

In a quilt that uses equal amounts of each color, as this one does, consider each family's visual weight. Warm colors appear heavier than cool colors. Use "warmer" colors (red-orange and red-violet) toward the bottom of the design and "cooler" colors (yellow-green and blue-green) toward the top. The choice for background fabrics also contributes to the design's visual impact. Light grays and taupe calm the clear hues I chose for this quilt. By the way, my inspiration yardage never made it onto the front of the quilt but made a beautiful backing.

Selecting the right fabrics from my stash took experimentation. I made far more Nine Patch blocks for the border than I actually needed and played with the  blocks on my design wall before sewing the rows together. I also cut out each appliqué shape in several choices of fabric to evaluate how the colors played with each other.

Taking pictures with a smartphone is a great way to quickly test value and color choices. It also helped that my husband has developed a great eye for composition and color through his own hobby, photography. We both rely on the other's critique.

Technique

The Nine Patch block's simplicity is deceptive. Strip-piecing helps speed the process, but the trick to matching hundreds of points is lots of starch, a thin line of basting glue, the finest straight pins, and accurate seaming. I used a small C-Thru® ruler to ensure each seam measured a scant ¼".

Once I was happy with the layout, I completed the border before working on the medallion center. Since the blocks were on point, I delayed trimming the Nine  Patch blocks along the quilt's edge until the quilting was complete. To prevent the border's bias edges from stretching in the meantime, I applied fusible seam tape along the edge.

Creating the Nine Patch appliqué blooms was so much fun, I ended up with more variations than room on the block. Again, starch and basting glue were key to making the ¾" appliquéd Nine Patch blocks. For other appliqué components, trimming oversize nine-patch units using freezer-paper templates was the easiest way to have the shapes evolve. Leave a generous ¼" seam allowance around each template when cutting, press under the seam allowances, and glue baste. The side edges of the basket were too bulky to turn easily, but a narrow striped binding was an easy solution and added interest.

I cut my medallion background fabric a generous 30" square and trimmed after the appliqué work was complete. Not only will the Medallion block shrink, but the border blocks may not be accurately sewn even by the most careful quilter. Measure the opening for the medallion in several places and take the average of the measurements. Add ½" to the width and height, trim, turn under the edges ¼", and appliqué in place.

My quilting choices were simple so as not to detract from the design of the quilt. I limited my tools to a walking foot and the BERNINA® Leather Roller Foot. This foot makes echo stitching around appliqués very accurate; and because the feed dogs remain up, there is rarely a tension issue.

My final technical challenge was the binding. To avoid covering the block points in the border, place the double-fold binding on the back of the quilt edge but sew from the front with your seam line just shy of the points. Then fold the binding to the front, touching the points. With a thin line of basting glue under the binding, press the binding into place. Hand sew the binding with tiny appliqué stitches.

The Blocks

Nine Patch Border Blocks: Cut 1½" strips from white/gray and colored fabrics. You need 34 blocks in each of 4 colors.

Nine Patch Border Squares: Cut 108 squares 3½" x 3½" from a white/gray print.

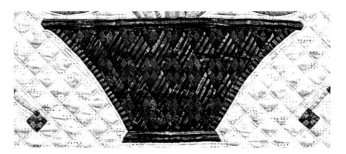

The Basket: Cut ⅞" strips of your darker and lighter colors. Cut strip-set segments at a 60° angle. Match the ¼" intersections carefully and sew your Diamond Nine Patch blocks together. You will need 23. Cut eighteen 1⅝" diamond shapes for the plain blocks.

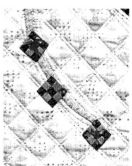

Mini Nine Patch Bloom: Cut ¾" strips. Fold the finished block's seam allowance to the underside and secure with basting glue. Appliqué to the Medallion block. Keep in mind that the medallion appliqué is meant to be whimsical, so accurate piecing is less important than with the border.

Left Nine Patch Bloom: Cut ⁷⁄₁₆" strips for the red and blue Nine Patch blocks. Alternate the 1¼" (finished) Nine Patch blocks, then trim to the shape of the appliqué.

Right Nine Patch Bloom: Make wonky Nine Patch blocks and trim to the shape of the appliqué. Have fun with scraps.

Middle Flower: The circles in this block are 5¾", 2½", and 1"(finished). Appliqué the smallest circle to the middle circle, turn over, and trim behind the 1" circle.

Set aside. Appliqué the petals to the largest circle, then attach the smaller circle unit on top. Turn over and trim. Arrange the mini blocks around the outside of the 1" circle to create a star.

Finalist
Claudette Booker

San Antonio, Texas

Meet Claudette

In the early 1970s, my grandmother gave a quilt top to me. "Aunt Clara" was a farmer's wife and had made the top from scraps, old clothes, feedsacks, and whatever she could find. I had never made one, but I knew that a quilt was a top, some batting, and some more fabric on the back. I think I pin basted it and, with a large wooden hoop, I started "quilting" it with a running stitch, now called the rocking stitch. I was hooked and made a few other quilts by hand, but supplies and information were very limited.

A few years later, America experienced a quilting revolution of sorts, inspired by the 1976 bicentennial. Suddenly, more books and fabric were available. It was an exciting time for quilters.

We were an Army family and moved from Louisiana to Germany in 1980. My quilting basically came to a halt. No one I met in Germany had heard of quilting and finding cotton fabric was almost impossible. The same thing happened when we moved to New York in the early 80s. However, a move to the Baltimore/D.C. area in the mid-80s was like finding heaven! There were some amazing quilt shops. I took some classes, joined a guild, and started entering my quilts in local quilt shows. I haven't stopped quilting since.

Most of my quilts are quite traditional. Maybe it's because I do most of my work by hand, both piecing and quilting. Maybe it's because I am drawn to traditional blocks and fabrics. I love the calming, traditional look of Civil War reproduction fabrics, but then I am also drawn to the vibrancy and joy of batiks and more colorful fabrics. They all find a place in my quilts.

We travel a lot and I love the portability of handwork. Several projects always travel with me (rarely fewer than four). If I get tired of working on one thing or technique, I can take a break and work on another. When I start a new project, I always think about how it will travel. I usually plan which projects are going with me long before I even start thinking about packing my clothes.

I make my quilts to be used. I make them because I am inspired by a pattern, a fabric, a technique, or something intangible that makes me want that quilt. I make them for my kids and grandkids. I want them to have something to remember me by. I like the idea I am carrying on a tradition that is centuries old. My quilts might not always be the most original, but I like putting a part of myself into my creations.

I am lucky that I am able to quilt all day, every day. My day isn't complete if I haven't picked up a needle and thread. Ideas for quilts are constantly running through my head. How do I fit quilting into my busy life? It's more like how do I fit my life into my quilting!

Inspiration and Design

I wish I could tell you that there was some long, drawn-out process that I went through when I designed this quilt, but I would be lying. This project developed when I wanted something easy to work on in the car. I dug through my stash and found a two-yard piece of black.

RADIANT RAINBOW

51" x 51"

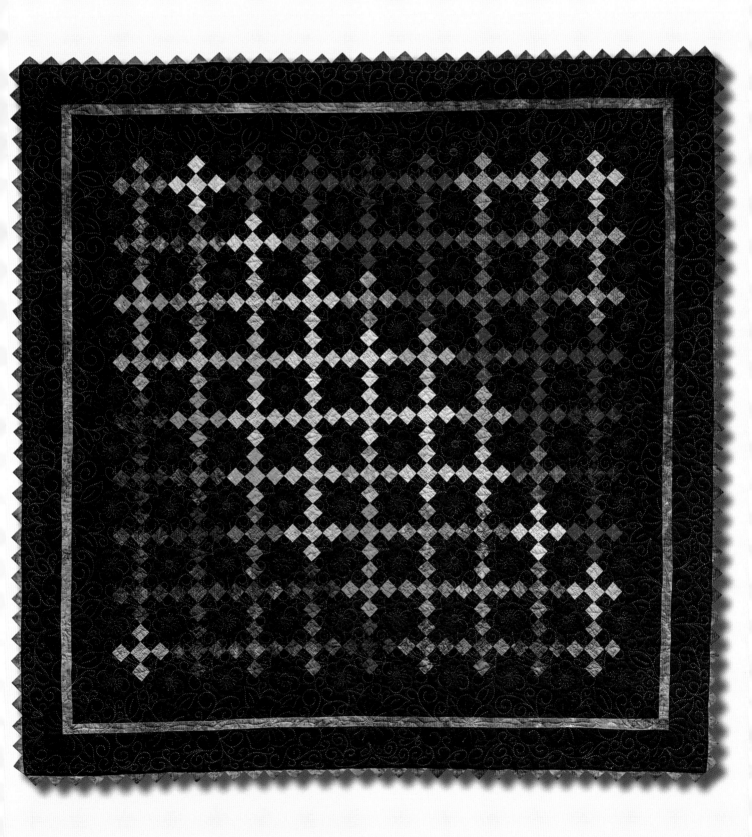

The Bali Watercolor Batik pieces were leftovers from another project. I have always been drawn to the graphic quality and quilting in Amish quilts and decided the batiks and black would make great Nine Patch blocks.

Using EQ7, I figured out I had just enough black for 81 three-inch Nine Patch blocks, alternate setting squares, edging triangles, and a 3" border. It would finish at about 45" x 45". Once all the blocks were finished, I started with a random layout. I tried a straight setting, but preferred them on point. Once I saw them on the design wall, I thought "Rainbow!" I rearranged them, beginning with reds and worked diagonally across the quilt to violet—you know, in a "Roy G. Biv" arrangement (the mnemonic for remembering the sequence of the colors—R=red, O=orange, and so on). I also worked from light to dark and back to light, with the lighter yellows in the center. Once I completed the top, it went into my pile of tops to be quilted "someday."

I must have been living under a rock for the last several years because I had not heard of the NQOF contest. Someone posted something about it on social media and I thought, "I have a Nine Patch!" I looked at the rules and discovered my quilt was too small. So, I started thinking about how to make it bigger. I went back to my stash and found three batik fat quarters that blended all my colors together. I added a narrow border of the batik and another 3" black border. Luckily, I was able to match and purchase more black fabric for that final border! Before I started quilting, the top measured 51" x 51".

I knew I wanted to hand quilt it fairly heavily with an allover design. I had the perfect stencils in my stash. (Have I mentioned that along with fabric, patterns, and books, I collect a lot of stencils?) I found two variegated threads that worked perfectly— multicolored and green.

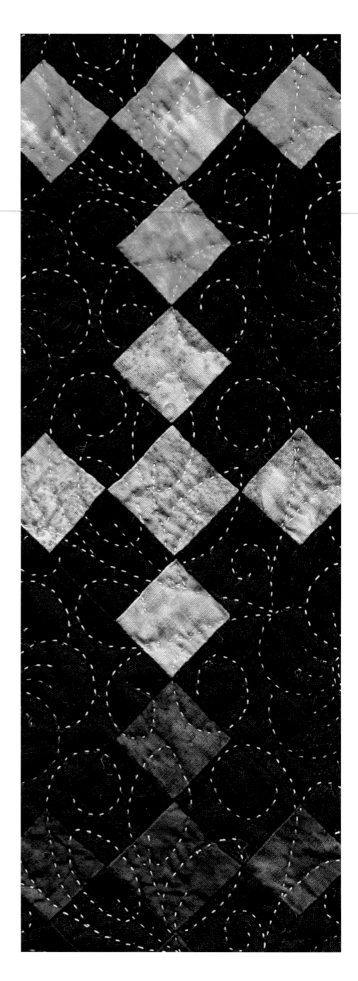

The basic stencil designs didn't provide enough quilting for me, so I added freehand swirls to fill in the blanks. The more I quilted, the smaller the quilt got; so it was back to the drawing board to figure out how to add a couple of more inches "just in case" it went below the required 50" x 50" size. Prairie points were the logical answer.

Back to my stash I went and pulled out the fat quarters I had used for the inner border. I had just enough fabric left to cut 68 squares for 1" prairie points. They added the two additional inches I needed!

Technique

I really enjoy hand piecing and hand quilting. I like taking my quilting wherever I go or spending most of my evenings sitting on the couch watching television while I hand quilt. Unless I have a specific deadline (like this quilt), I am usually not in a hurry to finish any of my quilts. They get done when they get done.

This quilt was specifically started so I would have something to work on in the car. We travel most of the summer and throughout the year, visiting family and grandchildren. I like to get everything cut out and marked before we leave home. To keep everything organized, I use a lot of plastic boxes of different sizes for my projects. I store the pieces for individual blocks in small plastic storage bags.

For this project, I cut my batiks into 1½" squares, five for each block. Because some of the colors were so similar, I pinned the pieces for each block together with a safety pin. Then I cut enough black 1½" squares for all the blocks. With those pieces, a spool of black thread, a needle, some pins, scissors, and a thimble, I was ready to travel.

To make traveling with my quilting a lot easier, I've purchased empty bobbin donuts and filled them with all the colors of thread I might need for a project. I like the little leather thimble pads instead of a thimble for hand piecing and appliqué. They are inexpensive and I don't care if they get misplaced. I made a small pincushion from two leftover 2½" squares and some scraps of wool batting. A metal gift cardholder or mint tin makes a good thread and scrap catcher.

I recently discovered cosmetic bags as useful containers for traveling with my quilting. They usually have two large pockets on each side and some kind of smaller pockets or dividers in the center. Oh, the possibilities!

The majority of my quilts are hand-pieced and hand-quilted. It is just something I really enjoy doing. I feel like a part of me goes into every stitch. I enjoy being able to take it wherever I go, even if it's just to another room.

There are some great books out there with instructions for hand piecing and hand quilting. My first "teachers" were Jinny Beyer, Ruby McKim, John Flynn, and many others. I read their books and learned all I could from them, adapting their techniques as I got more experienced.

So, cut up some fabric and pack the essentials. A lot can be accomplished in short bursts of time. One evening my husband asked me if I ever just sit. My response was, "Why just sit when I could be making something?"

Finalist
Diane Kay Evans

Forest Ranch, California

Photo by Amy Moffett

Meet Diane Kay

I was born in Washington D.C., but spent my formative years in Michigan where both sides of the family lived. My natural, artistic, crafty bent was fostered or influenced by different members of my extended family (but none was a quilter).

My grandpa was born in Canada and had built a cottage there on the shore of Lake Huron where we spent our summers. He liked to make things—all kinds of things. I was fascinated by a pillow he had woven out of leather strips (in fact I've promised my sister that I will try to make her one similar to it out of some deer hides her husband has sent me). I also had a love of dance, and he fashioned a hula skirt for me out of twine strands knotted onto a waist piece (rudimentary macramé). I loved it! He also gave me my first painting lessons and talked to me about light and shading. I know my grandma crocheted, but oddly, I never saw her doing it.

On my mother's side of the family, my aunt (and middle namesake) sewed. Boy, did I want to get my hands on that machine! I did get my first little machine and a pattern and fabric for Christmas when I was nine to make a dress for my Betsy Wetsy doll. All I remember clearly about that was the chain stitching coming out. Mom made sure I got a real machine by the time I was 12, even though she had no interest in sewing herself. Her creative talents were in the performing arts, where she's had a long and critically successful experience.

My dad has always been creative and inventive, but as I was growing up his time was primarily spent supporting a family of six. I especially liked a small chest of drawers he painted with each drawer wearing its own lovely soft shade of a color he had mixed himself.

Our family moved from Michigan when my dad was transferred. I always say, "I did 10–20 in New Jersey" (my ages there). We lived in a rural, wooded area. It was here I largely taught myself to sew, knit, crochet, and macramé. Only one of my three sisters shared a real interest in sewing and crafts. We had great times doing macramé in the backyard in bathing suits with our work anchored to lawn chairs. These days she'd rather design a kitchen than a quilt!

When I was 21, I moved to New Hampshire. At 23, two friends talked me into moving to California. As fate would have it, I met my husband within three months of that move. (Both friends moved back east within a year's time.) We married two years later and moved to Vashon Island in the Puget Sound. John's grandmother, Betty McDonald and author of *The Egg and I* and the Mrs. Piggle-Wiggle series, had lived there and we were looking for a change. We started our family there with the birth of our daughter, then moved to Forest Ranch where we have lived now for the past 30 years. Our three boys were all born in this area.

Most of the quilts I made when the kids were young were very basic patchwork with a poly batt. Few were even tied. In the mid-90s I saw my first art quilt in a *Threads* magazine and shortly thereafter an article on Michael James and his work. I still have the pages I tore out of those magazines. I'd never seen anything like it!

NOVA

53" x 53"

I started making some Eleanor Burns quilts and a bargello. In 1998, I naively entered a contest sponsored by a national chain store. I was chosen as one of thirty finalists, but didn't place. Here's that rough attempt.

Shortly after this, I started working in a fabric store where some of my coworkers were quilters. There were also a lot of quilt books to peruse. I joined the Annie's Star Quilt Guild (named after Annie Bidwell) in 2000. It's been an endless source of inspiration, and lessons from many well-known quilters have helped me grow in this wonderful field of endeavor. My first full-sized bed quilt, hand quilted on a standing round frame, was completed after 9/11. It was soothing to lay down those rows of stitches during that sad, trying time.

I love the world of quilting. It has so much to offer us all.

Inspiration and Design

This is the third time I've entered this challenge. I was lucky to be a finalist in the 2011 Orange Peel contest. The next year I entered but was not so fortunate. It's good to be back, and I'm looking forward to taking my parents to see the lovely town of Paducah!

I knew from the beginning of the challenge that I wanted to use a Blooming Nine Patch look in gradated shades. I'd made a quilt with commercial prints years ago from the book *Tradition with a Twist* by Blanche Young and Darlene Young-Stone. I loved the concept of color from one set of nine patches

blending over into the next round of squares. I also knew I wanted to use "hot" colors.

Back in the early 70s, I took a weaving class at the University of New Hampshire and remember being awestruck by the color combination I saw in a picture a fellow student had: fuchsia and tangerine…purple and melon. Those colors blew me away! I knew I had to use them someday.

I love hand-dyeds and have done some dyeing, but I'm far from expert. It's still a real hit-and-miss adventure for me. So it was challenging trying to get the color runs I was aiming for and I had to do a lot of re-dyeing. I discovered that my dyes really do have a shelf life and have become less viable as the years passed. Dyeing the purple appliqué was especially interesting. I wanted one big piece so I needed to dye it outside. I laid down large open plastic bags in my yard, sprayed the dyes on, and then covered it with more bags held down with rocks. The picture is from the second time I dyed it because the colors didn't have the saturation I was looking for the first time around. (It had rained during the night.)

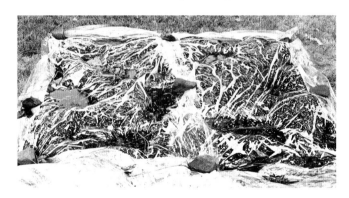

The concept for this overlay came from a picture I saw a few years ago in *Cutwork Appliqué* by Charlotte Patera. She'd done a small smiling sun appliquéd picture with rays that fanned from the center. To me, my quilt is evocative of a flower, roots, and the sun. I love doing what I call "big appliqué." I've done several large-scale flower quilts and plan on doing another soon, though none as large as Velda Newman's astonishing quilts. (I loved her class!)

These challenges are great because they give you a clear launching pad. I never cease to be amazed at where individual quilters go after "take-off." We all have such different visions. It's very cool.

Techniques

Typically in a Blooming Nine Patch, you can do strip-sets and cut them down to piece your squares. In order to get more randomness I needed to cut individual 1½" squares and put them on a design wall. It took a lot more time but helped me achieve the look I wanted. I also had to underline the lightest blocks in the center to get them looking their brightest. It made the hand quilting a challenge though. Lots of seams, lots of layers, lots of stab stitching!

I stopped doing the Nine Patch blocks and put in bigger pieces in the outermost part of the pieced area. Originally I'd intended this quilt to measure around 60" x 60". But when I started to draw out the overlay pattern and thought about transferring it to the fabric, I realized I needed to scale back so the pattern could fit within the parameters of my largest light box—my living room window! So, 53"x 53" is how it ended up! I used newsprint from end rolls and hand drew the pattern. You can see the pattern taped to my window before I taped the purple fabric over it, then drew around the outline of the rays with a light-colored pencil.

I centered and pinned the marked top and basted down the center of all the rays and around the perimeter. I cut away a scant ¼" outside of my drawn line a small section at a time and needle-turned and stitched. I find needle-turn appliqué well worth

learning if you love appliqué, because it's the fastest, most direct method.

Here's a picture of the back of the pieced quilt top, after it was appliquéd but before I cut away the fabric from behind the rays to reduce bulk.

For the quilting, I chose to machine stitch in the ditch around the rays. I hand quilted radiating circles out from the middle and also hand quilted fluid lines extending the rays to the edge. In this day and age of phenomenal machine quilting with all of its intricacies, I realize my quilting is very minimalist, but to me it exactly finishes what I'm trying to say with my quilt and doesn't flatten it out. I like the juxtaposition of the organic flow of the rays with the blocks and that I was able to get the color to glow.

Finalist
Cathy Geier

Waukesha, Wisconsin

Meet Cathy

I've been in love with quiltmaking for nearly 30 years, but I got into the hobby in the silliest way. I met an older woman at a county fair in Chesapeake, Virginia. I say "older woman" because I was in my 20s and she seemed pretty old. Now I realize that she was probably my current age! (Not old at all, merely aged, like fine wine and cheese.) I stopped and talked with her about her quilts and learned that she gave lessons. Up to this point in my life, my only creative hobby was counted cross-stitch. You know counted cross-stitch—you spend hours and hours and have four inches of color to show for your efforts. This lady's quilts were BIG. I got into the hobby because I could make something big. (I told you it was silly.)

I learned to quilt in the dining room of Fran's home. She taught me to hand piece and hand quilt and I loved it. It was a slow process, though, and after a couple of years I taught myself to use a sewing machine to piece. As my children were growing, I worked on traditional wallhangings, always finding a therapeutic peace and creative fulfillment through playing with fabric.

In the 1990s my interest in quiltmaking exploded when I began to see landscape quilts made from patchwork squares and triangles (watercolor and impressionist quilts). From that point on, I've been making landscape quilts. I love hiking and camping, and being able to capture a landscape in fabric is thrilling. I wrote my first book, *Watercolor Landscape Quilts: Quick No-Fuss Fold & Sew Quilts* (Krause Publishing) in 2005. I combined landscapes pieced from squares and triangles with raw-edge appliqué. My latest book, *Lovely Landscape Quilts: Using Strings*

and Scraps to Piece and Appliqué Scenic Quilts (Fons & Porter, 2014), is all about using strips and scraps to make landscapes.

My favorite part of quiltmaking is in the planning, designing, and the arranging of fabrics. I really don't like the piecing part. (Isn't that shameful, coming from a quilter?) To help me keep those straight rows straight, I developed a way to use a tear-away foundation, which I use when piecing squares as in INTERWOVEN. I also use it when I create landscapes made of pieced strips. I actually have a patent on this technique.

INTERWOVEN was the first traditional patchwork background I've made in years. I found it so much fun because of all the colors and the rhythm I was able to bring into the quilt top. While I still love the idea of making landscapes from long strips (the linear aspects of these quilts intrigue me), I have a feeling that there are more traditional-with-a-twist patchwork quilts in my future. From hand piecing Nine Patch blocks when first learning to quilt, to having one of my quilts in this exhibition, my life and my quilting are truly merged. I am interwoven with quiltmaking.

Inspiration and Design

This quilt came together through a series of small events that shaped my thinking over the months it took to string-piece the blocks. While some of my quilts are planned out precisely and then turn out as I planned, this was not one of them. This quilt was more of an experiment for me.

INTERWOVEN

53" x 53"

My idea began several months ago when I came across a graphic image of gray woven ribbons with an overlay of bright red poppies. I began to think about what weaves of color would look like. At the same time, I was in the process of cleaning and reorganizing my sewing room. For years I have tossed leftover fabric scraps into large boxes and shoved them under a table. (Out of sight, out of mind!) For the last couple of years I've been making strip-pieced landscapes almost exclusively; I had a LOT of leftover strips. I decided to spend a couple of months string piecing and using up my scraps.

After I had pieced the quilt top, I discovered that the blocks I had sewn were called Interweave and that the pattern was first published by Miriam Nathan Roberts in 1984, then used by Jinny Beyer and other designers for various fabric manufacturers. "Interweave," I thought and as I began to think about this word, I realized that certain aspects of my life are interwoven with my quiltmaking. I love making landscape quilts and have been making them for nearly 20 years. Part of this love for landscaping is because I see God's hand in the beautiful world around me. My quilt, INTERWOVEN, then became a vehicle through which I could express my joyful celebration of this interconnectedness I feel between God, this beautiful earth, and my quiltmaking.

The major challenge I faced in this quilt was designing the appliqués. I did not want to merely create dark silhouettes; I wanted more interaction between the tree, the trefoil, the woman, and the patchwork background. Therefore, when I designed the tree, I created open spaces in the branches themselves so the light from the patchwork would shine through them. I also used a variety of dark colors in the tree branches to reflect all the dark colors of the solid blocks in the Nine Patch quilt.

When I created the Celtic trefoil to represent the Trinity, I chose an open pattern in the circles to once again tie the symbol to the patchwork beneath it. I tied the figure of the woman with the background by

creating the illusion of light shining down on her and through her skirt.

I'm very pleased that INTERWOVEN was accepted into this exhibition. I hope that people who love to express themselves in fabric will identify with the joyful woman who celebrates color and texture and life through quiltmaking. (In case you are interested, I barely dented my pile of scraps!)

Technique

Several years ago, I hit the proverbial wall while sewing together the multitude of squares in a watercolor quilt. I simply could not sew one square to another any longer. Because of the bias stretch and the added bulk in seam allowances. I could not use the pre-printed fusible interfacing designed for watercolor quilts, "Necessity is the mother of invention" goes the old saying, and out of necessity I figured out a way to use a tear-away foundation to piece.

The gridded fusible product works because you fuse your squares of fabric within the grid pattern. Then you fold along those grid lines and stitch ¼" from the folded edge. It is a very fast way to piece a multitude of square patches. I adapted this idea of folding and sewing along the grid lines to use with a tear-away foundation. It is fast and accurate and the foundation is torn away from the seam allowances leaving a perfectly pieced quilt top with no extra bulk. Though it may be hard to visualize, this is the method I patented and will try to explain to you.

Using the largest rotary mat you have, a ballpoint pen, and your ruler, draft a grid on a tear–away foundation. The two products I use are designed for clothes pattern adjustments: 830 Easy Pattern® tracing cloth by Pellon® and Create-a-Pattern Tracing Interfacing by Bosal. Both of these products come on bolts and are 44"–45" wide.

This grid can be any size you choose. Simply line up your rotary ruler and draft a grid. The grid you draw needs to take the seam allowance into account, so if you draft a 2" grid, your squares will finish at 1½". Do you paper piece? If so, you'll see the possibilities for building a design within your drawn grid. By adding additional sewing lines you can create a variety of elements, for example an archway or a fence.

Once the grid is completed, use a glue stick and attach your fabric patches to the foundation. Keep the glue out of the seam allowances! Piece any triangles or rectangles within your drawn grid by flipping the foundation to the back and "paper piecing" along the sewing lines you drew. Trim off any excess fabric. Using a large needle (100/16) and tiny stitches, fold along the grid lines, and sew ¼" from the fold. Sew all the vertical or horizontal rows (one or the other) first. Then tear away the foundation from the seam allowances. From the back of the foundation, press the seams in opposite directions such that in sewing the next batch of fold/sew rows, your seam allowances will be nestled together in opposing positions.

Once the final batch of fold/sew rows is finished, the foundation can be removed from the seam allowances. Press the quilt top flat, add appliqués and borders if desired, then peel off the remaining foundation.

This method may be adapted to piece rectangles, squares with sashing and cornerstones, and long straight rows as in my strip-pieced landscape quilts. Any uniform pattern can be drawn, as long as the fold and sew rows are consistent across the length and width of your quilt. It is fantastic for creating scrappy quilts in the Irish Chain, Blooming Nine Patch, and Trip Around the World patterns.

Finalist
Julia Graber

Brooksville, Mississippi

Photo by Amy J. Graber

Meet Julia

I was born and raised in the Shenandoah Valley of Virginia along the banks of North River in Bridgewater. I learned to make my own clothes in home economics classes in high school. My parents had a fabric shop in Dayton, Virginia, where I spent a short time clerking in the evening. I remember feeling the fabric and dreaming of making quilts.

I come from a family of seven sisters and one brother. Each year, we have a retreat that includes four generations. For an entire week, we sew and quilt, paint, talk, laugh, and relax. We take our current projects and work on them, learning and gaining inspiration from each other.

I moved to Mississippi to teach school, and it was here that I met and married Paul Graber. We have five boys and one girl and now enjoy 10 grandchildren. We live on a farm near Brooksville growing cotton and grains, raising hogs, and are involved in a small trucking company. We are members of Magnolia Mennonite Church and enjoy the fellowship and activities of our local brotherhood as well as mission activities in Romania.

I made a few utility-type quilts soon after we were married and as the children were growing up.

It wasn't until after our youngest went to school that I really delved into making quilts, taking up the challenge of designing my own. In time, I joined a few of my sisters in a round-robin project. We each made a quilt center and passed it on to the next sister to add to it. In the end, we each had a quilt with a flavor of each sister in our own quilt. I taught a class of high school girls how to piece quilt blocks, then I began to spearhead projects for our church's sewing circle, making quilts for charity.

I have taught quiltmaking classes and fiber art classes in my home and at surrounding guilds. My love for the craft has grown with each quilt. When the Possum Town Quilters formed a guild in 2004, I joined as a charter member. They have provided me with lots of inspiration, encouragement, and challenges. I'm also a member of AQS, NQA, MQA, and SAQA.

I still like the traditional and scrappy large quilts, but recently I have been drawn to making smaller works in fiber, creating art quilts. I love the challenge of taking an image—whether from a photograph, nature, or my mind—and creating it with fabric and thread. My fiber art work is representational and often minimizes detail. It brings me joy when viewers of my work are drawn in for a closer look. I'm encouraged when they study the piece and discover with delight that it is not just another quilt but an expressive and compelling piece of fiber art.

I enjoy teaching workshops and giving lectures and trunk shows at different quilt venues. You may visit my blog, Life as a Quilter–Julia Graber (http://juliagraber.blogspot.com), to learn more about my life and quilting.

BUBBLED DOUBLE
NINE PATCH

63" x 63"

Inspiration and Design

I am challenged by taking an old familiar quilt block and turning it into something new and innovative with bright and bold colors. The New Quilts from an Old Favorite contest provides just that.

In the 2009 NQOF contest, I placed the traditional Burgoyne Surrounded block in an irregular grid with a strong black diagonal through the center.

I liked the outcome and decided to try the same technique with the Double Nine Patch block for this year's contest.

I enjoy using EQ7 to start the process and pick out the traditional block pattern and set it in different layouts then rotate, color, and flip the block to make many samples.

Technique

My BUBBLED DOUBLE NINE PATCH is made using only two different colorings of the same block. In studying the final layout, I decided that I needed four identical blocks of each size. I printed out the block in color to use as a guide.

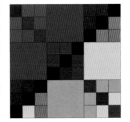

The center of the quilt consisted of 36 identically colored blocks in varying sizes that could be reversed or rotated. I started with the outside blocks and worked my way toward the center.

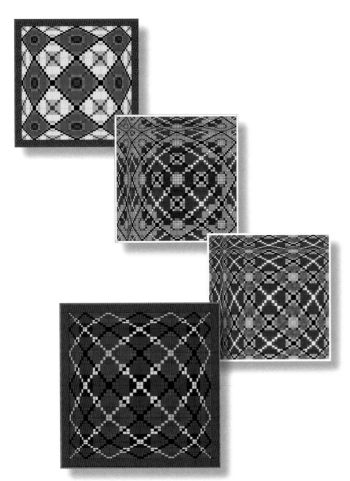

The border consists of 16 Double Nine Patch blocks that are colored with red on one side of the black diagonal and gold on the other. It is reversed and rotated from the original in varying sizes and helps create the bubbled look.

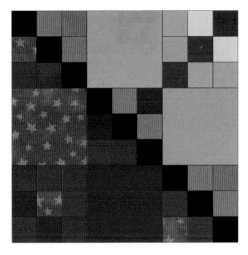

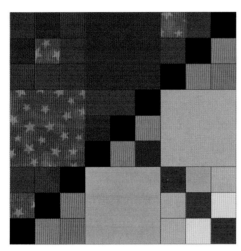

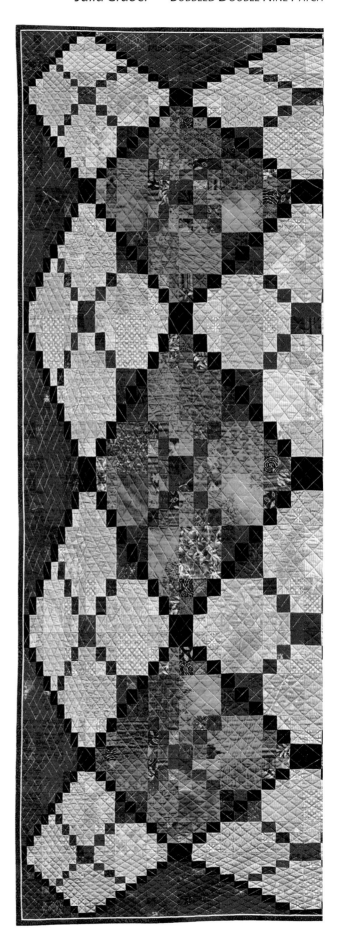

As in the Biblical account of the rich man and Lazarus (Luke 16:19-31), this quilt ties together Heaven's gold, Hades' fire, and water's coolness in an optical illusion.

Finalist
Anita Karban-Neef

Cary, Illinois

Photo by Lucia Rodriguez

Meet Anita

I've been quilting off and on for about 20 years, though in the beginning it was only a wallhanging or a table runner and other small pieces. My interest really gained momentum around 2007 when I started taking on small quilting challenges and entering contests. From there, it spiraled in many different directions including full-size bed quilts, art quilts, and more contests and challenges. I wanted to experience as much as possible and try new techniques.

Years ago, I looked at appliqué work and hand quilting and thought, "No way! Not for me." Never say never! I have since done machine and hand appliqué as well as hand quilting, enjoying all the processes. I may not have mastered them but I always took away some knowledge or skill.

I don't like to pigeonhole my style, though I have found my quilting "voice" comes through most strongly when I am basing my design on traditional quilt designs—Nine Patch, Double Wedding Ring, etc.—twisting them to be new and different or with pictorial quilts. I like to call myself a Traditonal-Twist-Modern-Art Quilter. As with most things, I find my work to be ever evolving. For instance, in the past few years, I've grown away from using all commercial fabrics to favoring more batiks and hand-dyed fabrics.

Where we live now, I don't have a large elaborate sewing space. I've claimed the family room as my studio and you can find me there whenever I have a spare minute or a dedicated chunk of time. Usually, that's with my Chinese Shar Pei, Drake, at my feet and the one or all three of our cats occasionally wandering

in to check my progress. For piecing, I favor using my Singer® Featherweights or Singer® 301A, while all my machine quilting is done on a 12-year old Singer® Scholastic 6510 mechanical sewing machine. I don't currently belong to any local guilds, as quilting is my way of having some quiet time with my thoughts, though I use my quilt blog to share my quilting adventures and really enjoy reading about others (cherryquilt.blogspot.com). I do try to travel to a few of the larger quilt shows each year, appreciating the creativity of others, getting reinspired and, of course, shopping the vendors!

I am fortunate to be able to travel from time to time to my parents' vacation home in Michigan, sewing machine and gear in tow, for some intense, dedicated quilting time. There, I commandeer the dining room table and indulge in marathon sessions. The idea of having to pack everything to travel forces me to really focus on a project to ensure I know and have what I need to complete it. It helps strip away a lot of distractions and quickly ends indecision. This is a special place to me, having visited there all my life, packed with memories and experiences. I find it very beneficial to go there if a project is stalled or needs to be finished for a deadline.

I am extremely lucky to have a very supportive husband, Wil, encouraging my quilt work. He's been called upon many times to take over all the household duties when I'm in a deadline time crunch, detour a road trip into a quilt shop, remind me to stop working and eat what he has cooked, and offer thoughtful advice or design/color opinions.

FIFTY-EIGHT NINES

52" x 55"

Wil is particularly sensitive to any unusual sounds coming from the studio—crashes, bangs, and the odd cursing fit. That's when he walks halfway down to the lower level and carefully inquires as to the source of the consternation. Most of all, he understands my need to create—that it sometimes overrides everything else in our lives—and patiently waits, knowing that balance will eventually come round again.

Inspiration and Design

This quilt started a few years ago, right after it was announced that the theme for 2015 was Nine Patch. At that time, while I didn't have even an inkling of what my design would be, I just knew I wanted to use blue batiks. So that set off an extended fabric shopping adventure. Wherever I happened to run into batiks for sale, be it at a quilt shop or a show, I'd grab a few fat quarters or a couple of half-yard cuts of something blue. My motto was, "Build the stash." That way I would have a large palette to choose from when the time came.

When the time finally did come, I had a pretty good selection, but unfortunately, I then decided I wanted to stay mostly in clearer blues–nothing smoky or grayed, nor too green or purple. That narrowed down the palette quite a bit and revealed some holes in the stash around the lighter end of the value scale. On the flip side, I had also built up the turquoise, teal, aqua, and green batiks for what ended up being the contrasting patches. The slight deficiencies made me really focus on design. What was a medium value became a light value when my dark values were

indigo. A few charm squares and Jelly Roll® strips filled in some of the gaps nicely.

My design plans are usually carefully thought out with swatch cards, color-coded to match my graph paper and colored pencil drawing, with a detailed fabric cut list. Not this time. This is what the "plan" boiled down to: a quick line drawing with the three colors defined by highlighter marker.

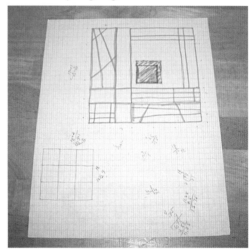

My quilt decided to evolve organically and somewhat backwards. I started with the complementary accent color Nine Patch block of nine patches—the reds, orange, pinks, and peach. With that piece completed and waiting to be attached to something, it was time to put the pedal to the metal and get the body of the quilt underway.

Still lacking a decisive plan, I started on the upper-left section. It wanted to be angled and long. To successfully piece this section, I chose to use a full-sized paper foundation of newsprint paper. Thinking I had it down pat, I stupidly cut the paper foundation completely apart instead of just into the wedge sections and proceeded to piece some of the patches to the wrong side of the paper! Not my most shining moment! But I did what any self-respecting quilter would do: take pictures of my mistake.

Upper-left angled section

After the struggles with the angled section, I changed tactics and focused my attention to the four green sections. Since these are normally neutral or lighter blocks in a traditional Nine Patch, I decided to make them all the same for continuity. The first thing was to find nine greens that I could shade from light to dark. The greens quickly morphed into teals, as those were brighter, clearer fabrics, already in the stash.

Teal cross-section

The width of the sections was perfect for the width of three 2½" strips. Here, my Nine Patches would be arranged horizontally into a strip, rather than a block. All I needed to do was vary the length of each patch so that the total length would cover each section required. To that end, the patches in the 12" section varied from 1"–1½", finished size. Suddenly, the quilt went from one to five sections complete—a huge boost to morale!

Five sections on the design wall

While the upper-left or angled section had light values, the majority of it was medium. That being the case, I wanted the lower-left section to hit light and dark values. I chose the Uneven Nine Patch block for this section as it related well to the almost square dimensions required. This section went together very easily!

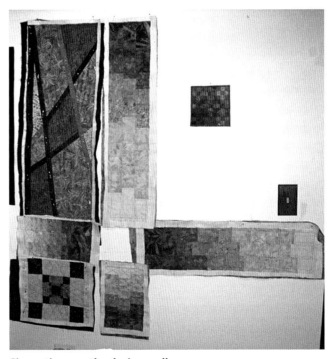

Six sections on the design wall

Around this time, I was having doubts about the largest section, the upper right, still as of yet un-designed. Originally, I had probably imagined that this would be the first section designed, as it would serve as the base for the accent piece. Yet, as I moved through the designing, this section ended up being last. Only afterward did I realize that the upper-right section needed to mirror all the other sections in its makeup.

Then I moved to the very center section, the blue twin of the accent color Nine Patch block of nine patches. This is where precut batik charm squares came in handy for getting the blend I was looking for on the transition from light to dark. They really filled in the gaps.

Once the center section was finished, I was looking to balance the angled section with the lower-right section. It was long and narrow but horizontal instead of vertical. I knew it couldn't be a traditional Nine Patch layout. I did two sections that way and wanted to also repeat the more subtle value change. The result was the "windows" section. There are what appear to be four windows sitting side by side. But in reality, each window was made up of two Nine Patch blocks. By setting them face-to-face, you lose the visual break because the light fabric continues from one Nine Patch directly into the other, as do the medium-value window frames.

I could no longer put off the upper-right section. It was time to tackle what would be the background for the accent piece. I wanted it to tie all the other sections of the quilt together but not overwhelm the accent piece by being too busy. And my drawing wasn't helping. So I started from the inside out! I placed the accent Nine Patch of nine patches in the same center position as its blue counterpart. It would be the center of the inner Nine Patches of this section. Since it would be hand appliquéd on top of the main body of the quilt, I put a piece of purple-blue batik on the design wall to hold its place, and stepped back to face a large blank space around it.

In order for the other eight patches not to compete with the accent piece, they had to be just fabric— not pieced in any way shape or form. Their size and placement needed to mirror the overall quilt layout and their values had to work with whatever I placed outside of them to fill in the whole quilt section. Quickly doing some quilt math and simple sketches, I determined that the upper-right section would be a Nine Patch (with a Nine Patch of nine patches in the center) within nine Nine Patches. (Try to say that three times fast!)

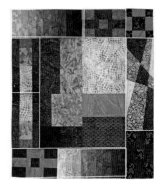

Upper-right section with divisions

It was easier to do than I thought. Once I sketched the layout and dimensions, I just needed to pick from the Nine Patch styles I used on the other section of the quilt, decide which one fit the space best, and repeat fabrics where I could. Once I had a pieced the top of this section, it quilted out very quickly, again copying quilting patterns from the other sections where appropriate.

The final design decision was the binding and I wanted to give one more nod to the Nine Patch theme. So I chose to use nine strips of binding, shading the values from light to dark around the quilt. That brought the total number of Nine Patches to fifty-eight and that's how this quilt got its name.

Quilting Technique

Since I didn't have a detailed plan for the quilt as a whole, I decided to tackle not only the piecing of each section individually but also the quilting. As I moved around the quilt designing and piecing the top, I immediately layered and quilted that section, creating this quilt using a quilt-as-you-go method. I've also used this method on bed-sized quilts to make it easier to quilt on a domestic sewing machine.

Teal sections quilted

Once I had a vertical column of three sections quilted, I pulled back the batting and backing and carefully joined the top layers together. I then trimmed the batting so the sections would butt together in the seam.

The backing fabric was trimmed to just past the seam allowance on one side. The other side was left about an inch wider than the seam allowance, so that it could be folded under, pinned, and hand stitched down.

FIFTY-EIGHT NINES has three vertical columns, so once each column was complete, the columns were joined together using the same method.

Here is the completed but as yet unbound quilt showing the edges of the joined sections. The batting

butted edges are actually closer together, but they had shifted slightly in this picture when I flipped the quilt over.

It is easier to handle the joining of the quilt top seams if the machine quilting does not go within a half-inch of the edge, though a little further away is better. Additional machine quilting can be added in the open area after the back seams are hand stitched down. If this is not possible, extra care needs to be taken during the joining; the extra layers of batting and backing, though turned back, can cause the top to shift and you end up with wavy seams.

By using the quilt-as-you-go method for this quilt, I was able to keep the project moving along while allowing the design process time to evolve. Since each section was quilted differently, I relied mostly on color and repeated fabrics to bring it all together.

Finalist
Zeeda Magnuson

Minneapolis, Minnesota

Photo by Lucia Rodriguez

Meet Zeeda

I started quilting in 1979 when I tired of cross-stitch and needlepoint. I needed a new challenge, which I tackled by electing to make a double-bed-sized Log Cabin using pin dots, solids, and one little calico fabric. The blocks were "wonky" and my seams were about half an inch. It was not a stellar quilt, but I was hooked! While I was taking post-grad classes, I landed a job at The Cotton Shoppe quilt shop in Richfield, Minnesota. The owner, Florence Zentner, also owned a warehouse business that distributed fabrics and notions to quilt shops across the country. She would host Meet the Shop Owners gatherings and invite nationally known quilters like Jinny Beyer. At the time, V.I.P. and Peter Pan fabrics retailed for $3.98 per yard, with muslin selling for $1.79. Oh, those were the days!

It was a thrill for me to meet and learn from the best early in my quilting journey. I was like a sponge, soaking in all of the tips and techniques being taught. I was soon teaching beginning, hand quiltmaking classes. I think it is very beneficial for everyone to hand stitch before switching to a sewing machine. Today, with the availability of specialty quilt sewing machines, longarm quilting machines, rotary cutters, specialty rulers, and specific threads made for piecing, quilting and embellishing, it is a wonderful time to be a quilter.

I remember being intimidated by hand appliqué for a long time, until I took an appliqué sampler class from Carolyn Sidebottom at Glad Creations in Minneapolis. After her class, I challenged myself to needle-turn appliqué the traditionally pieced Little Red Schoolhouse design, with all of its straight lines and tight corners. I thought it would be easier to appliqué than to piece all of those little components. It was an eye-opening challenge for me. While I still enjoy appliqué, now I primarily machine appliqué my projects.

Three and a half years ago I joined Minnesota Contemporary Quilters (MCQ), that reinvigorated me as a quilter with its inspiring members. Before joining MCQ, I never entered a quilt into a contest or quilt show. The group holds an annual themed challenge that is shown in conjunction with the Minnesota Quilt Show. The challenge quilts are then shown across the state at various venues. MCQ also sponsors a category in the Minnesota State Fair: A Quilt-on-a-Stick. In 2014, the theme was Ghosts, Ghouls, and Goblins at the state fair and I was fortunate to take home the first-place ribbon for my quilt SCARECHILD AFTER MIDNIGHT. Although I started late in my quilting career, entering local and national contests has been a great delight.

I cannot imagine a time when I will not be quilting. I enjoy every aspect of it, starting with the selection of fabric combinations, choosing the right pattern,

NINE PATCH CARNIVAL

53" x 53"

the right quilting pattern, and even putting on the binding, which brings the gratification of a finished project.

Inspiration and Design

Amish quilts have always been my favorite genre of quilting. I am drawn to the bold and vibrant colors, the simplicity of the patterns, and the emphasis on the secondary design of their beautiful quilting patterns. Recently, I have enjoyed seeing the explosion of the work of the modern quilters, with the open space within their quilts, the use of white fabric, and the simplicity of the design.

NINE PATCH CARNIVAL was my way of blending both of those genres. The title came from the twirling blocks that reminded me of my favorite carnival ride, the Scrambler, which takes the rider on a fast-paced zigzag pattern, with the cars moving on a back-and-forth path throwing the riders across the seat of the cars. The inner peak and spike border is reminiscent of the pennants hanging around the carnival tents, adding the feeling of festivity. The outer border of Nine Patch blocks is meant to be representative of the carnival goers arriving to join in the fun.

The biggest challenge for me on this quilt was creating the outer border. I wanted to make sure that those Nine Patch blocks would turn the corners evenly, so I had to use my math skills. I now wish I had enjoyed geometry class more than I did. After measuring, drafting, and making a couple of test blocks, I added two elements. One was simply adding an extra inch to give extra depth to the inset triangles that create the top and bottom of the Nine Patch border blocks. The second was adding a row between two Nine Patch blocks. With these changes, the outer border seems to float around the quilt, which I think works well.

One thing that I like about the quilt is the staggering of the blocks, creating a secondary zigzag design between the rows. I can see using this technique again in another project. A second aspect of the quilt I really like is the shading of color. I used Cherrywood

fabrics that are so much fun with which to work and play. Cherrywood dyes a myriad of colors, as well as creating great shades of each color. The fabric looks like suede, and when I am quilting it on my home machine the needle goes through it effortlessly. I think it would be fun to recreate this quilt with a black background showcasing a carnival at night. The light or pastel fabrics would really "pop" adjacent to a solid black.

The size of this quilt works perfectly in my home. I like to display quilts all year long, changing them out frequently. I use curtain rods with clip rings to hold quilts at the binding. It makes it so simple to switch out quilts for holidays, special occasions, and for the seasons. Friends and family enjoy coming over to see the various quilts on display.

Technique

I would recommend paper piecing to anyone. This is ideal for quilts with lots of sharp points like Mariner's Compass or New York Beauty. It is a method that has been used for decades, but quilters of today now have great tools available to make it even easier to be successful. You can get great results and can accomplish seemingly difficult patterns with this technique, making a beginning quilter look like a veteran.

I have been using lightweight foundation paper as the base, which makes removing it easier than if using copier paper. Good quality tweezers will assist you in removing the little pieces at the seams. Reducing the stitch length also helps perforate the paper, which makes it easier to remove and less likely to loosen the stitches. I use a glue stick to attach the first piece of fabric to the pattern to provide a solid base from which to start. This was particularly important to NINE PATCH CARNIVAL because the middle of the block was patched and not just a simple piece of fabric. In addition, a light box was crucial for aligning the Nine Patch block to the center of the paper-pieced foundation block.

My advice in paper piecing is not to rush. Start the project when you have time to pay attention and when you will not be distracted or interrupted. The use of a "Do Not Disturb" sign on the outside of the quilting studio door may help. It is easy to get confused as you get started, but once you have your process down, you can really move quickly and obtain great results.

When quilting from a commercially produced pattern, quilt in the order of the numbers printed on the pattern. When making this quilt, I had to predetermine the stitch order that would make the most sense and create the least amount of angst. Did I want to start at the center and work outward or did I want to start at one end and work toward the other side? I determined that with this quilt, I had no choice but to start at the center and work outward.

Another suggestion is to not fear "wasting" fabric. To keep your project moving forward and to avoid having to pull out your seam ripper, cut your fabric larger than you think you will need. This will address any issues related to having too little fabric available to stitch the next seam. It is easier to trim away the extra fabric than to add the $\frac{1}{16}$" of fabric that you are short. Don't fret if you make mistakes. They will happen. Just have your seam ripper at the ready, or start over with the block. Using a larger-sized piece of fabric will also allow you to throw out the small scraps in the yard for the birds and squirrels to use in their nests and to create a colorful neighborhood!

Enlarge 200%

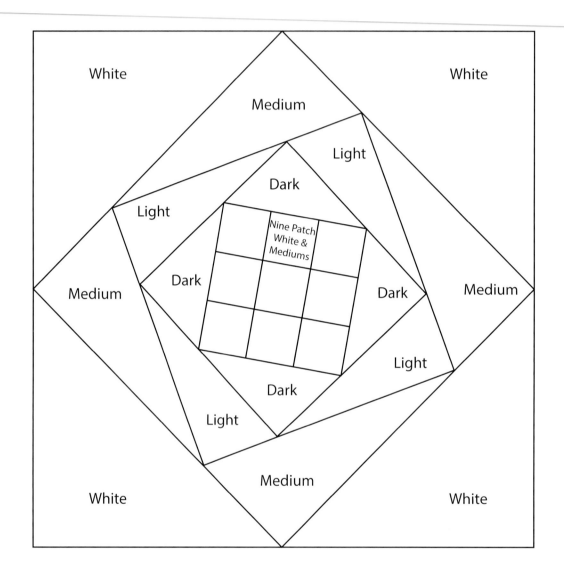

Pastel Nine Patch Template
3¾" nine-patch centers (finished)

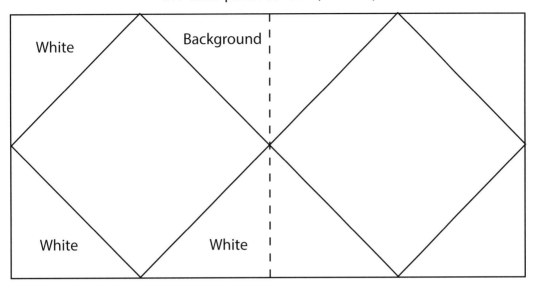

Nine Patch Inner Border

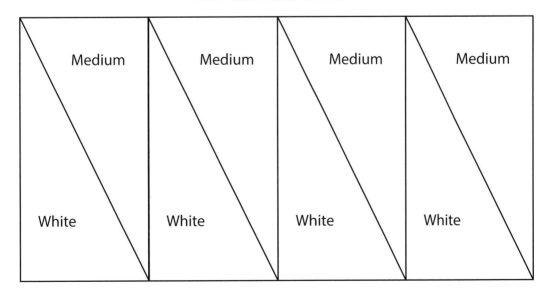

Finalist
Judy Martin &
Grinnell, Iowa
Lana Corcoran
Cedar Rapids, Iowa

Pictured on the left, Judy Martin and on the right, Lana Corcoran.

Meet Judy

As a child, I was fascinated by my mother's sewing machine and my father's graph paper, probably because they seemed to spend so much time engaged with them. I sewed doll clothes on the sewing machine at the age of nine and stitched my own clothes in junior high and high school. I made my first quilt as a college student, using dressmaking scraps and my little Singer® Featherweight. I'm still excited about quiltmaking.

Quilting has provided my livelihood since 1979 and my husband's livelihood, as well, since 1988. I have been a quilting magazine designer and editor, a quilting instructor, lecturer, and quilt book author. In all this time, I have been fortunate to look forward to going to work every day. Quilting is my creative outlet. My favorite parts of quiltmaking are designing the quilt, selecting fabrics, and hand stitching the binding. All the possibilities at the start of a new project excite me, and the completion of a quilt fills me with an incomparable sense of accomplishment.

For the first 20 years of my quiltmaking I designed using my beloved graph paper. When I got a home computer, I began designing using Adobe® Illustrator® software. Rather than using graph grids, I now make precise computations based on geometry, algebra, and sometimes trigonometry to create accurate scale drawings of interrelated shapes. I have patterned more than 1000 original block and quilt designs in my 22 books and scores of individual patterns and magazine articles. My color and fabric choices range from traditional to Asian and even modern.

My designs are often informed by a traditional aesthetic. I usually incorporate scraps and pieced borders in my quilts. I am fascinated with secondary designs, such as the arrangement possibilities in Log Cabins. I work loosely in series, with one idea leading to another. I can see myself adapting the border concept from Skewed Nine Patch for a future quilt. Perhaps I'll revisit the happy color scheme in another quilt one day, too. As long as I continue to have new ideas for quilts, I'll keep on designing and stitching.

I hope that someday quilters will once again have the pleasure of making the full range of designs in our quilting heritage. Right now, the emphasis seems to be on shapes that are simple to rotary cut or paper piece. I am comfortable using templates when needed, but perhaps some new cutting tool will one day make kites, skinny half-diamonds, and other odd shapes easily accessible to all.

Skewed Nine Patch is my 251st quilt, made in my 45th year as a quilter. However, it is just my second contest entry. I am happy to have it make the finals of Nine Patch: New Quilts from an Old Favorite.

Meet Lana

It's really a wonder that I started quilting at all.

When I was about six, my parents gave me a child's hand-crank Singer. Try making anything on that, much less little doll clothes, with a six-year old's coordination. My mom showed me what was possible. She sewed and made beautiful clothes for me, as well as two twin wholecloth quilted

SKEWED NINE PATCH

77" x 77"

bedspreads. In high school came the requisite ugly dirndl skirt, which served as the foundation for the pleated trousers, blouses, and an Eisenhower jacket that I made for myself.

Remember the quilted Japanese-style jackets of, um, a few years ago? I started my foray into quilting with one of those. Intent on making a garment that no one could tell was homemade, I researched how to quilt. Or so I thought. I learned that the most difficult part of making one of these jackets was keeping the three layers—top, batting, and lining—from slipping as they were quilted. I thought I had found just the technique, adapting the newly available fusible web as the method to keep them together. I bonded the top to the batting and then the lining to the batting. The quilting was beautiful. Unfortunately, I had also created the fabric equivalent of plywood. The jacket was great if you wanted to keep your arms straight out at your sides. It was stiff as a board. It was there that I discovered ripping out (un-sewing). I took it all apart, picked out the fusible, and made it again without it. I still have that jacket.

I started quilting quilts thanks to a very patient and generous new quilt shop owner in Gaithersburg, Maryland. She gave of her time and provided suggestions for preserving three old family quilts that had been used, and unfortunately misused, sometimes, sad to say, by me. I felt guilty about taking her time, so I asked what I might do if I wanted to make a quilt. She suggested I start with a Nine Patch. That took about 10 minutes and I was ready for more.

Since then, I've probably made about 30 quilts of various sizes. One of the last ones I made was an oversize king for my husband. I knew how I wanted it quilted, and I knew I couldn't do it on my domestic machine. So I got a longarm and I fell in love with longarm quilting.

For the last 11 years, I've been quilting almost exclusively for others. I quilt nearly every day, generally for about six hours a day. I've done thousands of quilts—pantographs, freehand, custom, and show quilts. My customers have won over 50 ribbons for quilts that they have pieced and I've quilted. But I enjoy quilting the everyday quilts, as well. I love seeing the look on my customers' faces when they see their quilted tops. Tops just seem to come alive once they are quilted.

I've never tired of longarm quilting. Each quilt is different and has its own set of design possibilities and technical requirements. It is necessary to understand how fabric behaves and which threads, colors, batting choices, and quilting plans will work best for the intended use of the quilt as well as the quilter's budget. Add machine maintenance and repair to that list. And last, but not least, it is important to remember customer satisfaction and good business principles. There are always new patterns, methods, and tools to keep quilting fresh. For me, quilting continues to be both challenging and satisfying.

There are several of my own tops waiting to be quilted, some UFOs, and many more still in my mind, influenced by quilts I've quilted and various other sources. I'm also especially inspired by other quilters, both traditional and modern. One of these days I hope to use that inspiration on my own quilt tops. Right now, my customers' quilts come first.

Like many quilters, I've had previous careers. People might enjoy knowing that I was a photojournalist and nominated for a Pulitzer Prize. I started out with newspapers and ended my photography career as a wire service photographer and a member of the White House Press Corps based in Washington, D.C. There I covered President Reagan, flying with him on Air Force One. After that, I changed direction, received my MBA from Wharton and worked in business process engineering for several large corporations.

Inspiration and Design – Judy

My original vision for SKEWED NINE PATCH underwent seven revisions before I completed the quilt. The traditional Nine Patch block provided the starting point for the design. My first inclination was to try skewing the block to form either 60-degree or 45-degree diamonds. After seeing both, I settled on the 45-degree diamonds and began to try different colorings and arrangements. Early in the design process, I decided to color each Nine Patch block from two values of the same color, with five bright diamonds and four somewhat lighter ones. This would define the boundaries of each block and emphasize the Nine Patches. My palette never strayed from the orange, pink, violet, blue, turquoise, lime, and white of my initial drawing, though the placement of the colors changed several times.

The most challenging part of the design for me was coming up with a suitable border design for this complex, multicolored quilt. I really surprised myself by selecting an appliqué border. I am a big fan of pieced borders and I have never used appliqué in any of my quilts before. The amount of appliqué in the quilt is really minimal, but its impact is major. The border is my favorite part of this quilt as it provides a simple frame and counterpoint to the straight-line piecing.

For my initial quilt design, I started with a small Lone Star arrangement in lime and turquoise. Then I added Broken Star elements in pink and orange, followed by two rings—one of blue and violet Nine Patches and another of lime and turquoise blocks. By using analogous colors within each star or ring, I hoped to make each star and ring look cohesive and stand apart from the other areas. I added a zigzag border of Nine Patch blocks in pink and orange to finish the first version of my quilt design. This medallion version did not seem innovative enough to me, but I had some other ideas to try.

Since the Nine Patch blocks had fewer diamonds than most Lone Star units, I decided that I could make multiple Broken Stars without the quilt becoming too large. This would result in a more complex and unique quilt. For the second version of my Skewed Nine Patch, I omitted the outer ring and repeated the medallion four times. I added a small Lone Star to the quilt center. I adjusted the colors, and changed the border corners, as well.

Still not entirely pleased with the quilt, I changed the border block colors for the third version.

For the fourth design variation, I omitted the stars in the border corners. When these small changes did not produce the results I had hoped for, I could see that I needed to make a more substantial change.

For the sixth iteration of my SKEWED NINE PATCH design, I omitted the appliqué stems and leaves and made the background outside the Nine Patches green. I also switched colors in the Broken Stars and the outer rings in order to follow the sequence on the color wheel. Where the green background met the black border, I exaggerated the serpentine quality of the vine from the previous appliqué border. Finally, I changed the border Star Flowers and three-eighths Star Flowers to consistent three-quarter Star Flowers. At last, I felt I was getting somewhere.

For the fifth version of my design, I centered the first Broken Star medallion and surrounded it with three-quarter medallions. This gave the quilt a stronger focus. I changed the background outside the diamonds to black. In a real departure for me, I decided to try an appliquéd border instead of the pieced one in an attempt to make the quilt more interesting. However, this looked too busy to me.

In the seventh sketch, I tweaked the design minimally, simply changing the green background back to white and the outer border from black to blue. I also reintroduced the appliquéd stem as a way to add a color accent and simplify construction.

The eighth and final version of SKEWED NINE PATCH switches colors in the stars and rings. I maintained the colorwheel sequence, but I started with the warmest colors (pink and orange) for the star center; the darkest colors (blue and violet) were used for the inner Broken Star ring; and the lime and turquoise were used in the outer ring. This seemed to me to put the emphasis in the right places, and this is the sketch that guided me in piecing the quilt.

Inspiration and Design – Lana

Judy and I have collaborated on about 20 quilts, this one being the latest. We each bring our own design and technical experience to the table. Judy generally has a rough idea of what type of designs she would like on her quilts. As a longarm quilter, I am more familiar with how the quilting will be accomplished. For example, one of my main concerns is ensuring that the quilting enables important elements to be enhanced and that the quilting density is even and allows the quilt to be flat.

Judy and I met initially for about two hours to discuss possible designs for the quilting. We made about five pages of sketches, culminating in a sheet that listed each discrete block and the thread to be used. The initial plan was for feathers on either side of the appliquéd stem and in the orange and pink Nine Patches as well as the lime and turquoise blocks, echo quilting in the blue and violet Nine Patches, double arcs and quarter daisies in the cream squares, and curved grids in the background.

It was apparent that several things needed to be modified or further defined. Since Judy and I live about 80 miles apart, I emailed several new ideas and necessary changes to Judy and together we decided on the plan revisions. For example, the quilting of the feather motif for the orange and pink Nine Patches would be much too dense as initially drawn. In addition, I thought it best to digitize the design so that all feather motifs in the blocks would be exactly the same.

It became apparent that the cream background area was too irregularly shaped for any kind of grid, so I devised a pebble and curl fill motif. Judy still liked the idea of a curved grid, so I adapted one from *Shape by Shape Free-Motion Quilting with Angela Walters: 70+ Designs for Blocks, Backgrounds & Borders* (C&T, 2014) to fit in the lime and turquoise blocks. I adapted another of Angela's motifs to substitute for the echo quilting in the blue and violet blocks. I modified all of the block designs for consistent density and also digitized them for consistency.

On all our previous quilts, we have always agreed on the quilting plan. This quilt was a little different in that there was one area upon which we didn't initially agree—the background fill. Judy was concerned that pebbles would be so dense that the background would look "thready." However, she said that if I could do them "without looking too thread-covered, I'm okay with it." Thank you, Judy, for trusting me, as I think the pebbles make those blocks "pop." (Judy: I was entirely pleased with the quilting. Lana was right about the pebbles.)

Once all the block pattern designs and thread colors were agreed upon, I sent Judy a detailed summary of all the quilting that was to be done, and the quilt was quilted according to the plan.

Techniques—Judy

Nearly all of my quilts have been made with a pattern in mind. S\ KEWED\ N\ INE\ P\ ATCH is not one of them. Some of the background patches are unusual shapes and sizes. Furthermore, the combination of piecing and appliqué on the border and extending into the background of the quilt center is too convoluted to describe. As I made the quilt, it felt like every part of the quilt's perimeter needed to be done first, and yet it could not proceed until some other part was done. I utilized partial seams here and there, but rather than being at one end of the seam, most of the parts to be stitched later were gaps left in the middle of seams.

Generally I like the freedom to use scraps and make each unit in a quilt unique, rather than repeating the same fabric placement. For this reason, I prefer rotary cutting individual shapes to strip piecing. Initially, I cut diamonds and pieced them in three rows of three to make the Nine Patch blocks for this quilt. However, I found myself doing too much seam ripping and resewing to match the intersecting seams perfectly. As I had a limited number of scraps for this palette, I decided to try strip piecing after making just a handful of blocks. I cut 18" long strips from fat quarters and half-yards of fabric, cutting parallel to the selvage along the lengthwise grain. This allowed maximum stability of the fabric grain. It

also allowed for maximum scrap variety. As I needed more than eight units of each color, I made strip-sets out of several different fabric pairs in similar colors.

To help me align my units for stitching, I cut one end of each strip at a 45-degree angle and trimmed the point off using the "C" trim of my Point Trimmer tool (Judy Martin's Ultimate Rotary Tools). I found the joints easier to match with the strip-pieced units, so I strip-pieced the remaining diamond-shaped blocks.

As diamonds (or the strips for strip-piecing them) are cut based on their width plus seam allowances, and the background squares are cut based on the length of the diamonds' sides plus seam allowances, one of those dimensions was not going to fall precisely on a regular rotary- cutting ruler. I cut the diamonds using a regular ruler, and I cut the background squares using the Omnigrip™ On-Point™ Ruler by Donna Lynn Thomas.

I toyed with the idea of setting in all of the background squares around the Nine Patches. I have no qualms about set-in seams. In the end, however, I opted to split all of the Broken Stars (including their outer rings) into quarters, thus dividing some of the background squares into two triangles. I felt it would be unwieldy to set in squares while wrangling the entire quilt center. As the corner Broken Stars were three-quarter units anyway, this made perfect sense. The entire quilt center can be pieced from rows of one-quarter-Broken-Star units. (Note that the four corner Broken Star quarters are different from the other quarters. The central Broken Star quarters and the remaining eight quarters of the outer Broken Stars include one-quarter Lone Stars in two opposite corners. Each corner quarter has a single one-quarter Lone Star.)

The three-quarter Star Flowers in the corners of the border are made with one-quarter Lone Star blocks. For the three-quarter Star Flowers at the center of each side of the quilt, the half Lone Stars are part of the blocks forming the quilt center. The remaining two Nine Patch blocks forming these three-quarter Star Flowers are pieced into the quilt's border.

I cut the light background fabric that forms the inner border to extend all the way to the edge of the quilt. I placed the blue borders face up over the face-up light borders, aligning their outer, straight edges. I pin-basted and stitched the two border parts together ⅛" from the serpentine raw edges of the blue border. I then cut 8 seamless lime green bias strips 1½" wide for the stems. I folded the stem strips in half lengthwise, right sides out, and stitched each stem with a ¼" seam allowance. I pressed the stems to hide the seams and seam allowances beneath the stems. I pinned the stems, centering them over the serpentine raw edges of the borders. After hand appliquéing both edges of the stems to the borders, I tucked the

ends of the stems into gaps I left in the stitching at the center of each three-quarter Star Flower. Then I machine stitched over the gaps on the back side of the quilt and trimmed off the excess light background fabric around the quilt's perimeter.

Finalist
Susan Mogan

Mobile, Alabama

Meet Susan

I have been quilting now for almost 10 years. It's funny, but when I was younger I hated quilts. I am a bright color person, and the only quilts I had ever seen were all faded or made from muted colors and they didn't appeal to me at all. About 10 years ago, I began seeing quilts in fabric stores that were made in bright new fabrics and had a great color impact–"not your grandmother's quilt," so to speak—and that is when I got interested in quilting. I had sewn some when I was younger, and while I knew my way around a sewing machine I was no expert. I took a beginner's quilting class in 2005, bought a bunch of batik fabrics, and have been having a ball ever since.

I do not have a particular style, although almost all of my quilts are art quilts, and they are all original designs. I only make wallhangings and do not make my quilts to be functional or washable. Since I am too impatient to work by hand, I do everything on the machine except the binding. That same impatience means I am not good at following "quilt rules." I'll do whatever is going to achieve the look I want in the least amount of time. Since I get bored easily, I'll usually try something new with each quilt I make.

I actually do two distinct styles of quilts—original pieced designs and wholecloth painted and dyed quilts that are heavily embellished with needle felting, yarns, and free-motion stitching. I recently finished my first improvisational quilt and this is my first modern quilt. In 2015, my plans are to make a photo-inspired quilt of my three kids, another painted quilt, and then hopefully an entry for next year's New Quilts from an Old Favorite contest.

I am interested in learning to paint on silk with dyes, since I love the vibrant colors that can be achieved on silk, so my next painted and dyed quilt will probably be on silk. I enjoy taking classes that either enhance my design skills or teach me a new technique (my next class is Sue Benner's Expressive Painting with Thickened Dyes), and I also take art classes. I believe that all forms of artistic growth enhance each other and strengthen creativity, and I enjoy being around other artistic or creative people, whatever their area of expertise.

I moved to Mobile, Alabama, in 2013 from Paducah, Kentucky. I sure miss the Paducah quilt show and being able to go into The National Quilt Museum any time I wanted, but it will be a thrill to know my quilt is hanging there!

Inspiration and Design

I knew that I wanted to do a contemporary quilt, not necessarily a true modern quilt but something definitely not traditional. I also wanted to work in only solid fabrics, which I had never done before; I usually work in batiks. I had taken a class earlier this year taught by Rosalie Dace at the Quilt Surface Design Symposium on quilts inspired by the artwork of Wassily Kandinsky, so I decided to use that as my starting point. In addition, I had a group of blocks I had made in solid colors that were inspired by some blocks in Bethan Ash's book *Vibrant Quilt Collage: A Spontaneous Approach to Fused Art Quilts* (Interweave, 2012), and I wanted to include them.

I drew out my intended design on paper and started working. However, as I began making the sections of the quilt, I quickly found out that while I liked my

MODERN NINE PATCH

70" x 70"

design on paper, I hated it when I put it up on my design wall. I think part of the problem was the colors I had used (the one block reminded me of Good & Plenty® candy. While I liked the two corner blocks on their own, when put together in the quilt, both the colors and the traditional style clashed with the abstract style and clear colors of the center focal block.

I was so frustrated I almost quit entirely, but I decided instead to just scrap my original design and work visually from the center out. I kept the center section and the group of nine geometric blocks, and just let the quilt speak to me about what should come next.

I like a lot of color and have to remind myself to make some quieter areas to avoid having the quilt be too busy or loud, so I used grays as contrast. I originally had the appliquéd shapes straight, but I decided to angle them to play off of the angled shapes in the center block. I also thought the tilted shapes had more energy and looked more playful. Finally, I thought the quilt needed some darker areas to anchor it more, so I added the long triangles as frames for the center.

I was pleasantly surprised by the way the quilt turned out. It was not at all what I had started out to make,

but I liked the color impact and the bold, graphic look of the design. The size of the quilt gave those elements even more impact. Working in solids was a learning experience for me: I learned that I needed to use a larger scale and fewer pieces or the quilt looked fragmented and too busy. This quilt is different from any other quilt I have ever made, but it was an excellent learning experience and I love the finished product.

Technique

After discovering that my plan, which had looked so good on paper, looked awful made up, it was time to scrap the design and start again! I usually work visually from a starting point out. In the first photo, the upper-left section was made, and I was still experimenting with the set of nine smaller blocks in the lower left, as well as the sections with the appliquéd shapes. Note that at this stage the appliquéd shapes were still square with the edges of the quilt. Only when I was hurriedly moving them around and some of them were off-kilter did it strike me that angled shapes had a lot more movement and energy.

Construction continued. The lower left was mostly finalized, the lower right was beginning to take shape, but the center focal block was not in its final form. Very little was actually sewn together yet. I used about three boxes of pins to hold everything onto the design wall.

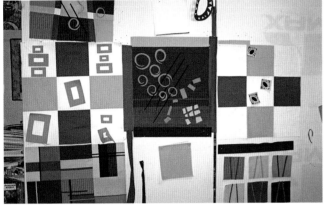

I tried out various layouts for the appliquéd ovals using paper versions (see photo below), and at this point the whole section was on the right side instead of at the top center where it ended up. As I worked on the quilt, I came to the decision that since the four corners and the center were all bright and mostly warm colors, I would do the interspersed sections in cool colors for contrast. The cool-colored appliquéd shapes and the gray squares ended up being a nice counterpoint for the brighter sections.

Most of the major sections are completed.

The last photo shows the top all pieced together before the appliquéd shapes were added. At this stage I had not yet decided on the dark triangle accents, and the top does not have the visual weight that the finished quilt has. I machined quilted the entire quilt with my walking foot, and used mostly 30-wt. thread so that it would show up more. The final look of the quilt was both a surprise and a delight!

(P.S. I did not include a photo of my original design because I think with some minor modifications it can still be a great future quilt, so I want to keep it under wraps for now.)

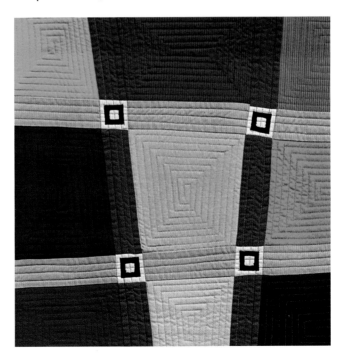

Finalist
Claudia Clark Myers

Duluth, Minnesota

Photo by Tom Myers

Meet Claudia

I love to make things. I love to figure out how to make things. When I was working in the theater, that's pretty much what I did—talk to the director/choreographer, get an impression of what they wanted, make the costume sketches, figure out how to make the costumes come out like the sketches, and make sure they fit the actor/dancer/singer and allowed them to move around. Most of the pieces I did for opera were headpieces or hats.

Opera singers usually wear wigs, not because they don't have any hair, but because they don't have larger-than-life-hair to go with their larger-than-life stage personae and costumes. So, their hats and headpieces have to be made from scratch. So, what do you make them out of? If you work in a full-fledged costume shop, you have access to buckram, wire, Fabri-flex, and all manner of professional materials.

If you are in northern Minnesota, before the advent of online shopping, you improvise. The first set of La Bohème hats that I made for the Baltimore Opera, I used wire window screening with the edges wrapped in masking tape to keep from cutting myself.

I thought the pros in the costume house would know that I was a novice and laugh themselves silly. Instead, I found out that they were blown away by my construction methods. The screening made the millinery extremely sturdy. That was in 1978. They may still be using that set of hats!

My point is that there were no instructions on how to make a flat tutu or how to make a Claudette Colbert-type Cleopatra headpiece—with a (rubber) snake.

NYNEPATCH PUZZLE

60" x 60"

How do you make a Father Time costume with a grandfather clock on the actor's head? How do you make a climb-able tree out of a wooden stepladder, a two-by-four, and a cardboard box? Well, you just have to figure it out, just as now I enjoy figuring out how to paper piece a Poinsettia block. Next time around, I'm going to be an engineer. I'm also going to be tall, thin, and beautiful. Next time.

About My Quilt

As I was thinking about the Nine Patch block and designing the first draft of the Flower block and the quilt layout, I began to see more and more possibilities to turn the different elements into Nine Patch configurations: the petals of the flowers, the ribbon design—all were possibilities. So, I decided to make a puzzle out of it. I love jigsaw puzzles anyway, and I work on at least one online puzzle every day.

My version of the ever-popular Nine Patch contains 57 Nine Patches. Can you find them all? Just in case you get tired of looking, here they are:

1	the entire quilt
5	each Flower block
4	each Ribbon block
5	the centers of the flowers, including the checkerboards
5	the inner center (orange, yellow, black) of each flower
12	each black and blue checkerboard
20	each flower petal
5	the quilt stitching in the orange center of each flower
57	

Congratulations, if you found them all!

Techniques

I have recently developed a new (to me) way of constructing a quilt. I call it "working on the wall." I piece the background, add the borders if there are any, and hang it up on my design wall. Then, I piece or appliqué the block elements or designs and machine appliqué or fuse them to the background. I either do raw-edge fusing finished with a close satin stitch, or turn the raw edges, glue them, and stitch down with an invisible stitch on my machine. If the pieces are small, I fuse them. If they are large, I turn the edges and trim out the background fabric behind the appliqués. This technique was used for my quilts MAGNOLIA and RED FEATHERS, and now NYNEPATCH PUZZLE.

MAGNOLIA

RED FEATHERS

It's a very freeing way to work, giving me the

opportunity to change not only the settings, the positions of the blocks, and other features, but also if I find I don't like the background, I can start all over and make a new background before anything is stitched or fused down.

I would like to tell you about a few "tricks" that I incorporated into NYNEPATCH PUZZLE that I have learned along the way—some from my years in stage work, and some from my quilting experience.

Notice that the background colors range from orange to gold to yellow. I placed the brightest, lightest yellow behind the center block, both to make it important as the center of the quilt and also to draw your eye inward. I also used this brightest yellow in the centers of all the Flower blocks and for some of the ribbons in each Ribbon block, so your eye would rotate around the quilt.

Three of the flower motifs have black-and-blue checkerboard Double Nine Patches and the remaining two have black. This relates them to each other and, even though I made the flowers different sizes and different shapes, you see them as similar and not disjointed.

Three of the flower motifs have little "orange slices" on the leaf edges, to integrate the Ribbon blocks and the Flower blocks. I like people to look at my quilts for as long as possible and think about them, wondering, "Why the heck did she do that?"

To enhance the idea of the quilt being a puzzle, I didn't sew the different elements of the Flower block together, but appliquéd them onto the background with a little space between the pieces, so they would look like the puzzle was still being constructed. I outlined everything in black satin stitch to emphasize their separateness.

I made the blocks different sizes to add interest and get you away from the same-block, same-block, same-block appearance. I also broke the seam lines of the blocks and let the flowers infringe on the blocks next to them—again, for interest and to give the quilt a looser, less formal feeling. The result is more creative and playful, less rigid.

Finalist
Annette S. Reynolds
Grove City, Ohio

Photo by Lary N. Lee

Meet Annette

Early in my adult years, I became thirsty for a higher education, so I enrolled in college for the first time when I was in my mid-thirties. I immersed myself in studio classes at the Columbus College of Art and Design in Columbus, Ohio. *Afterglow* was made while I was there, when I had access to printmaking equipment and a studio. I've often thought of translating it into a quilt and probably will someday soon. After three years majoring in fine art, I became interested in anthropology and other disciplines; so I transferred to The Ohio State University, where I graduated cum laude with a degree in art education. I cherish those years in college as a "non-traditional" student. I was challenged by the energy of the younger students and their uninhibited willingness to think and work outside the box.

***Afterglow,* serigraph by Annette S. Reynolds**
Image inspired by the West Virginia mountains

The most valuable critique I ever received from a professor was that my drawings and paintings lacked value contrast. I corrected that in short time, and the understanding of that design element is very helpful to me now in my quilting.

There are 14 quilters in my extended family. Being a painter, I remained on the periphery of their creative efforts until one day I "hit a wall" in my painting. In 2008, my husband and I had moved to Texas for a temporary eight-month stay. I took my art supplies with me and intended to paint uninterrupted for the entire time. It didn't work out that way. I was uninspired and unable to produce anything worthwhile.

One day, on a whim, I stopped in a quilt fabric shop and was overcome by the beautiful and colorful fabrics. I made a small purchase and went back to our apartment, not having any idea what I was going to do with the fat quarters. I began to rip the fabric in small squares and realized then that I would make a quilt. The next day, I returned to the shop and purchased a pair of scissors, some needles and thread, and more fabric. I hand sewed the ripped squares onto some cut squares leaving the raw edges exposed, and so began my first quilt. When I returned home after our eight-month stay, I entered the quilt in a local exhibition and took an honorable mention. From that time forward, I was "hooked." Fabric has become for me another rich medium with which to paint.

Each year, my family has a quilting get-together in our home town in West Virginia. In honor of our grandmother, Georgie Barnhouse, we named our gathering the Barnhouse Bee.

We come together to show off our new quilts, exchange blocks, catch up on family news, sing and dance to some bluegrass music, and eat lots of good food.

DRESSED TO THE NINES
51" x 51"

We were looking at my quilt, YOU ARE MY SUNSHINE, when we all spontaneously broke into singing the song.

In 2014, we had 57 relatives in attendance who came from Florida to Canada and several states between. It has been fun to meet the second generation of cousins—many who now come and have learned to appreciate their heritage.

Gathered at the Barnhouse Bee

In short, quilting has become the catalyst for maintaining our family relationships and extending the love we have for each other. This is the primary reason that quilting is important to me.

My husband and I have been married for fifty-three years. He has always been my best fan and has helped many times with projects that were too cumbersome for me. He often made suggestions that were insightful and appreciated. We have two grown sons, now with their own families. One family lives in Texas, the other in Colorado. We make frequent visits to them and take along our little dog, Gina.

Inspiration

DRESSED TO THE NINES was inspired primarily by the traditional Nine Patch pattern itself. It was the first quilt pattern I learned to make, and so it was naturally dear to me. It is such a humble design, but can be expanded many different ways to become very complex and interesting. I chose to retain the simple design and to dress it up with beautiful fabrics. I had some pieces of colorful hand-dyed satin fabrics that I decided to use, and I searched for other fine silk and cotton fabrics to complement those colors. After gathering my supplies, I made some sketches of how I wanted the quilt to look, but being frustrated with my drawings I threw them all away. I pulled out the sewing machine and just started stitching. From that point on, I worked intuitively, trusting my sense of color and design.

Artists can find inspiration almost anywhere they look. Most of us have the innate ability to see beauty in the mundane and the spiritual in God's creation. My family and my background as a child of Appalachian heritage have always been sources of inspiration from which to draw. Absence of monetary wealth often demands resourcefulness, and resourcefulness fuels creativity. I grew up with 11 aunts and uncles on my mother's side of the family in West Virginia. As children, we learned to create our own toys from things that we found around us. We made whistles from pawpaw tree limbs, paints from crushed soft stones found in the creek, playhouses on large rocks in the woods, and used canning jar lids for toy dishes, to name just a few.

My grandmother was always sewing something and I watched over her shoulder many times, learning skills I employ today. In the summer, when it was hot in the house, she sewed on the front porch, with morning glories and climbing roses growing along the banisters. She enjoyed the beauty of the country and cherished each child and grandchild. She was also a spiritual person and I feel certain we were all protected from harm because of her faithful prayers.

Georgie Barnhouse

All of us went on to become artistic in some way or another. My mother had a beautiful stitch and was especially talented in embroidery. Two of my uncles became talented musicians. Two other uncles created beautiful and coveted handmade knives. My Aunt Adah (Adah Lynch of Clendenin, West Virginia) became a well-known and respected watercolor artist, and it was she who made the hand-dyed and painted satin fabric in my quilt. My sister, Marsha Beane, is a beautiful and prolific traditional quilter. She encouraged me (I should say pushed me) to enter this contest. She brought the application back from Paducah, gave it to me, and insisted that I make a quilt for this contest. She believed in me and encouraged me throughout the entire project.

My husband, Gary, and my two sons, Jim and John, have always inspired me in ways that are indescribable. Their love, patience, and encouragement through the years always sustained me when my work was less than what I wanted it to be.

In addition to my family, I find inspiration in the natural world. There are patterns everywhere in nature and I am always looking for them.

Technique

The individual blocks were foundation-pieced on cotton/wool batting using the stitch-and-flip method. The batting prevented the satin and silk fabrics from slipping while sewing. I carefully selected the colors for each block in order to complement the hand-painted fabrics. I focused both on value contrast and chromatic contrast.

I machine quilted and hand quilted the blocks before they were joined. Then I attached all of the beads by hand and added a little tacking.

After making all the blocks, I had no idea how to put them together. I remembered a demonstration in my guild about a process called quilt-as-you-go and thought that might work. I made some test blocks, practiced a little, and went for it. Needless to say, it was quite a leap of faith for me to endanger my already completed blocks to a method of construction with which I was inexperienced. But it worked, and I was pleased with the results. As a final touch, I added more beads and quilting.

Finalist
Jan Soules

Elk Grove, California

Photo by Gary Soules

Meet Jan

I was born and raised in Rhode Island. I am the eldest and only girl in my family and had five brothers. I lived in a working class environment where my parents worked hard to provide the basics. Lots of frilly dresses for me and my dolls were not in my future. Out of necessity, I began sewing.

I loved sewing so much that my parents even bought me a brand new Singer® machine as a high school graduation gift. I worked my way through college and earned a teaching degree. Soon came marriage and two children—a son, Khristian, and a daughter, Keather. I started making them matching outfits the first couple of years and then I began what I call the second phase of my life. In the space of ten years, I lived in four foreign countries and enjoyed traveling and the finer things in life. Sewing took a back seat. In fact, I gave up sewing during most of the 70s, 80s, and 90s. In the 80s the family relocated to California, and I have been here ever since.

In the year 2000, my married daughter was expecting a baby girl. She asked me to make her a quilt. I felt a bit overwhelmed, but loved being asked. I got out my Singer® and tried my best—I can only describe the resulting quilt as "sad." However, reentry into my old pastime was all I needed. Within a month, I signed up for quilting classes and bought a new BERNINA machine. I credit wonderful teachers as helping me on my journey, especially the ones I experienced on my annual vacation to the Empty Spools Seminars each spring. I now call myself a quilter or perhaps a quilt artist. I began with traditional patterns and have grown along the way. I still enjoy paper- piecing and

hand-appliqué projects, but the bulk of my work has become more creative.

Having lived and traveled extensively, inspiration is always close at hand. My memories of the wonderful places I have visited can now be seen through each new quilt. In the past few years, I've traveled closer to home. I have enjoyed several visits to the Grand Canyon and have made a series of about five quilts based on it. Nature appears often in my work, especially in landscapes. The California landscape provides added inspiration as seen in WINE COUNTRY, one of my favorites, and SPRING FEVER. I love piecing my skies! It's become one of my favorite parts of my landscape quilts.

WINE COUNTRY, 46" x 47"

SPRING FEVER, 57" x 50"

I was lucky enough to be chosen as the featured artist at my guild, River City Quilter's Guild, in 2011. That experience exposed my work to a wider audience and I got the chance to teach and lecture as a result. I have a second career now that I am retired, and I just love it. I talk specifically about "Spectacular Borders," and use my quilts to point out options for borders that may be overlooked. I also teach a few workshops. My husband, Gary, is my driver, quilt holder, and companion. There is no way I would do it without his

POSSIBILITIES
51" x 51"

support. He enjoys meeting all the quilters as much as I do.

This is my second time as a finalist in the NQOF contest. I hope the contest continues as it offers quilters a chance to use a traditional block in a contemporary way. The diversity in each person's quilt is amazing!

Inspiration and Design

I was fascinated by the idea of the Nine Patch contest. It seemed like such a simple block. So how could I challenge myself to make a spectacular quilt incorporating this simple pattern and yet fit it with my desire to make something unique and imaginative?

Coincidently, earlier this year I attended a lecture given by Jean Wells at a local guild. Previously I had purchased her book, as I was impressed by her methods. Her freeform cutting and piecing style was something I wanted to explore. I came home from the lecture motivated and determined to give it a try. I retrieved the book from my library and began the process.

I tried one of Jean's suggested exercises. I started out making small 6" blocks in a Log Cabin manner and inserted tiny curved strips. I liked the results, and ended up turning four sample blocks into tiny pincushions. Now I had the beginnings of an idea for my Nine Patch project. Each block could be a small Log Cabin block with a solid center.

To tie my blocks together, I felt I needed a wonderfully unique fabric as a jumping off point. I was fortunate to find what I needed at a quilt show in Richmond, California. A vendor, Ananse Village, from Fort Bragg, California, was selling African fabric. Typically, I would just walk right past, as I didn't need to start collecting another type of fabric. I already had a large and varied stash, consisting of hand-dyeds, Marcia Derse fabrics, Australian, Japanese, Civil War, novelty, etc. However, since a close friend had just returned from a trip to Africa, I decided to see

what was offered. I was immediately drawn to two unusual African wax prints. They were relatively small pieces, not much bigger than fat quarters, but the colors were bold: lime and red. I knew I had found my starting point.

When I got home, I laid the fabrics out on my large cutting table and started pulling other fabrics to go with them. It was fun seeing the palette develop. One print had a touch of blue, which I decided I would use sparingly as an accent. That meant a trip to a quilt shop. I found the exact blue and even picked up a few more prints to add to the mix. I eventually added some black and white for contrast.

I love working with lots of color and fabric choices. That's always been my favorite part of making a quilt. I probably had too many options to begin with, but I like to edit as I work. I like to mix my fabrics, as a painter blends his brushstrokes, to see what happens as the colors and patterns touch each other. It's an unplanned surprise. As the designs take shape, the color choices became key to the desired effect.

This project was exhilarating from the fabric choices to the block design. I finished with a funky style of quilting, which I would describe as playful. I hope you enjoy my quilt story!

Technique

After assembling all my fabrics, I was ready to make my quilt. I had a vague idea of where I was headed, but only that. I like to create as I go, so usually I only have an idea and it changes on the way. For each Nine Patch block, I began by making a freeform Log Cabin-style block. I used about a 6" x 6" square of the focus fabric for the center and then added various sized strips around it. I did not measure anything, just added strips and trimmed. Occasionally I inserted a narrow blue strip as an accent.

Once the block was big enough (about 16" x 16"), I stopped and made a second block to coordinate with it using similar fabrics. When the two Log Cabin blocks were completed, I trimmed them to about

15½" x 15½". Then I cut them evenly through the centers horizontally and vertically. Now I had four pieces from each block, eight total. For the ninth piece, I cut a square from the focus fabric to be placed in the center of the design.

Now the fun began. I laid the nine blocks on the design wall and moved them around the center focus fabric. There were so many design "possibilities" that it was hard to choose the best arrangement. I spent a lot of time on this phase, as I feel it was critical to the flow of the quilt.

Each of the four Nine Patch blocks was made in the same manner—two with the larger print and two with the smaller print. The finished blocks are about 20" x 20".

After the four main Nine Patch blocks were done, I tried several setting options, with and without sashing. I was mindful of the contest size requirements and the need to comply. I ended up using one of my favorite black-and-white stripes as a sashing to divide the four blocks. It really made the Nine Patches stand out.

Since I lecture on borders, I like to "practice what I preach." I used different size and different motifs on two sides of the borders. I like to say,

"The borders are one of your last design opportunities; don't waste them." I had fun making the unique borders. For the scrappy pieced border running along the top and right side, I gathered all my remaining fabric and sewed strips together making a new fabric.

Then I subcut it into strips, joined them, and had a unique border that worked well with the vibe of the quilt.

I made small Nine Patches for the other borders and set them on-point. I used several of my green fabrics to frame them. I finished the quilt using a very free style of quilting. I think it further highlighted my desire to keep this quilt down-to-earth and simple.

I hope you enjoy my quilt and that you make your own. Remember the "possibilities" are endless.

Finalist
Sue Turnquist

Tifton, Georgia

Photo by John M. Kreger

Meet Sue

So many quilts and so little time. That is the mantra that drives my creative process at the moment. There are new designs, new techniques, and new quilts continuously swirling in my head, and it's time to follow my heart. I began quilting in 1993, the same time I started my career as a veterinary pathologist. I've juggled the two seemingly opposite ends of the spectrum for many years while sometimes losing track of my creative side. There is a history of familial Alzheimer's disease on my dad's side of the family tree. While my fate is still in question, I am exquisitely aware that time is precious, and I want to spend as much time as possible immersed in the creative process.

By the time this book is published, I will have begun the next chapter in my life. Excited and a little scared, I will be officially retired as of December 2014. Veterinary pathology has been a wonderful occupation and I have enjoyed every phase of my career. I will miss my job but I look forward to having more time to devote to quilting, reading, and playing with my Border Collies, Petey and Shelby.

Immediately upon retirement, the first thing on my agenda will be to sell my house. I adore my southern friends, and I would live in southern Georgia again if I had a "do over," but I miss the four seasons where I was raised. My eventual landing place has not yet been determined other than the Midwest. Arkansas and Missouri are at probably the top of the wish list. It goes without saying that my new community will have a quilt shop and an active quilt guild. With any luck, there will be an interesting running/biking trail, a good dog agility training facility, and close

proximity to excellent fishing and kayaking water. Heaven forbid that I should have a boring retirement.

Inspiration and Design

RED HOT SUMMER was designed and constructed during one of the hottest summers on record in South Georgia. The heat and humidity were stifling—perfect weather for staying inside and quilting! Many years ago, I acquired several yards of gorgeous hand-dyed fabric from a vendor at the Paducah quilt show. Over the ensuing years, I regularly unfolded and petted the fabric and promised I would feature it in a project someday. When I discovered that the theme for this competition was the Nine Patch, I was sure that this would be the perfect opportunity to use this coveted fabric. I planned the fabric placement as I sketched the grid pattern.

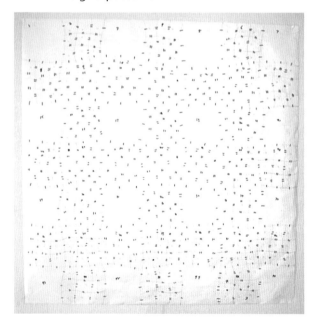

I ironed the freezer-paper templates to the chosen fabric and the blocks began to take shape on my

RED HOT SUMMER

60" x 60"

design wall. I auditioned three rows before I realized that I really didn't like the way the quilt was developing. The beautiful hand-dyed fabric fell flat once it was cut into roughly 2½" squares. In my frugal youth, I would have forged ahead and hoped for the best, but my older and wiser self opted to go back to the stash and start all over again.

I might as well admit that I'm a batik junkie and that I have enough batiks in my stash to open a fabric store. I dove into that glorious stash and pulled out a multicolored focal piece for the grid background and chose a lime green floral for the light patches in the Nine Patch blocks. The darks turned out to be an assortment of purple batiks and an orange-red batik.

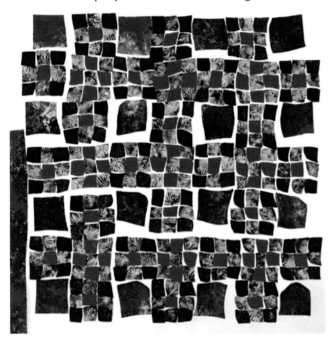

When possible or practical, I like to use several fabrics of similar value instead of a single fabric. The extra texture adds zing and interest. The original quilt was going to consist of the nine-patch grid with an appropriate border, but the regular horizontal setting also fell flat. It made my heart flutter when it was rotated so the grid was on point (and when my heart flutters, I pay attention), but then I had to design setting corners. I decided to carry the grid motif to the corners and add some squiggly curves that reminded me of heat wave. It struck me that the colors and heat waves were a good reflection of that miserable summer weather.

Technique

As a fledgling quilter, I was taught applipiecing, a curved piecing method by Caryl Bryer Fallert, and many of my quilts employ this method. The pattern for the center medallion was sketched on a large piece of freezer paper. (I was ecstatic when I discovered a source of 48" wide freezer paper but had no idea how heavy the roll would be.) Black registration marks were placed on the seam lines of the paper pattern to assist in reassembly. The paper pattern was cut apart on the seam lines, and the templates were ironed to fabric to facilitate auditioning on a design wall. Assembly began after all of the final fabrics were chosen. The components were assembled utilizing the registration marks, a light box, and Scotch® tape to join the seams in preparation for sewing.

Briefly, liquid starch was applied to the seam allowance with a Q-tips® swab and the fabric was turned to the back of the freezer-paper template with a hot iron. The light box was used to align adjacent pieced templates (using registration marks on the templates), and the tape was used to hold the aligned pieces together for stitching. The taped units were stitched together with invisible thread (Sulky® invisible is my favorite) using a tiny zigzag stitch that just caught the very edge of the folded-under top fabric. Neutral cotton thread or invisible thread was used in the bobbin.

I never intended for the center medallion to be set on point, so when the piece demanded this setting, I had no idea what to do with the corners. I sketched corner after corner before I settled on the wavy design that reminded me of heat waves. Similar to the center medallion, the first setting corner was sketched on freezer paper, and this corner served as a pattern to trace the remaining three corners. Having finally settled on a corner design, fabric selection was the next obstacle. While sorting through fabric, a summer striped batik fabric caught my eye. I adore striped batiks and I wish fabric companies would produce more of them (hint, hint). By placing the templates strategically on the striped fabric, I soon realized I could create a secondary design (yahoo!).

I recently took the plunge and purchased a longarm quilting machine, and this quilt was going to be the first real quilt finished on the new machine. As actual quilting time got closer my feet got colder, and I eventually resorted to the home sewing machine that I have used for quilting for so many years. The top was anchored with extensive ditch quilting, and then each patch and block in the center medallion was free-motion quilted with a whimsical sun design. The name was decided before the quilt was finished, and the label was printed on fabric that had been ironed on freezer paper and cut to 8½" x 11".

Finalist
Karen Watts

Mayhill, New Mexico

Photo by Don Watts

Meet Karen

Quilting has been an obsession of mine since 1991, when I made my first quilt—a sampler using a bunch of fat quarters and the book *Quilts! Quilts!! Quilts!!! The Complete Guide to Quiltmaking* by Diana McClun and Laura Nownes (McGraw-Hill, 1988). I had learned to sew as a child on my mother's 1949 Singer® Featherweight, which had been her first anniversary present from my dad. That Featherweight sewed everything: suits for work, dresses for ballroom dancing, drapes in our home, boat cushions made of vinyl, and upholstery for our couch. The one thing it hadn't sewn was a quilt, but it had been passed along to me and that's what I used it for.

I learned to piece and machine quilt on that machine but bought a new machine with a few more features a year or two later. Our daughter learned to sew on it as a child as well. Now, this Christmas, the trusty Featherweight is being passed on to her, newly graduated from college and living on her own. I wonder what that machine will sew next?

During my 23 years of quilting I've enjoyed experimenting with different techniques. Most of my favorites involve working with a machine, either sewing machine or longarm, but recently I've begun doing some hand embroidery working with wool. There's something very satisfying about using felted wool, maybe because I don't have to turn the edge under! I've taken needle-turn appliqué classes, but confess that I'm not a fan.

Another new technique I'm playing with is thread painting. In Houston this past November, I took three workshops on threadplay. Two of the classes used a sewing machine (Pam Holland and Jennifer Day), and the third was on the longarm (Sue Patten). They were fun and it was interesting to learn the differences between the processes each teacher used. Other teachers I've really enjoyed are Katie Pasquini-Masopust (using a watercolor painting as inspiration for a quilt); Sue Benner (fused collages and abstraction); and Ricky Tims (improvisational piecing and overall inspiration).

Looking ahead, there are plenty more techniques to try. I'm interested in trying to use fabric paint to embellish after the quilting is done. It sounds scary, with the possibility of ruining your quilt after it's essentially done. Still, I've seen some beautiful examples and will give it a try. I'm also considering branching out (gasp!) from quilting. I've often wished to learn more about photography, and in 2015 Ricky Tims is offering a 52-week photo challenge class. The class will run for a full year, and each week will include a lesson with video and a challenge fulfilled by a photo that each person will take and upload. Lessons will include camera techniques, photo editing, and composition. It's quite a commitment, but what an opportunity for learning and fun!

Inspiration and Design

CHASING SUNLIGHT was designed in a completely different way from my other original quilts. Generally I have a completed, or mostly completed design, before I start stitching. In this case, I had a general idea of a center medallion made up of nine Nine Patches with no rulers allowed! I started with a pile of Ricky Tims' hand-dyeds in blue, turquoise, and green, then added commercial prints and batiks for

CHASING SUNLIGHT

65" x 65"

variety. I wanted each "square" of the Nine Patches to be pieced as well, so I began by strip piecing some units, then cutting them apart and inserting other fabrics, however it happened to strike me. Cutting deliberately wavy lines with a rotary cutter was easy and sewing those gentle curves was not very difficult, either. But what I discovered was that the bigger the pieces got, the wonkier they became.

I completed the nine Nine Patches, but it became obvious that adding the long pieces of sashing between them in the same manner would result in a very unflat quilt top. My solution was to lay the blocks on a grid drawn on Ricky Tims' Stable Stuff® Poly, then to fuse and buttonhole stitch the black-and-white sashing pieces on top. When it was time to design the corners of the medallion, I attempted to piece them the same curvy, improvisational way, but that did not go well. Consequently the corners have straight seams, but with all the other curves in the quilt I figured that didn't matter.

I knew I wanted to add appliqué but what would it be? About that time my husband finished a song he wrote and recorded—*Chasing Sunlight*. I've always loved suns, so I drew a large curvy sun for the middle, with funky flowers for the corners. These are all fused and machine buttonhole stitched.

By the time I got to the border I knew I didn't want to piece long curvy strips. Instead I freehand cut just one of the border fabrics and laid it on top of the other one, fusing and buttonhole stitching them together. I made my little black-and-white Nine Patches (they have straight lines too!) and pieced them into my border strips. The tiny flange of orange inside the binding added a little pop of color that was needed to complete the look.

As for the song, a couple years ago I purchased a set of StoryPatches (www.stkr.it) while at the quilt show in Paducah. These are little iron-on QR codes that allow you to attach a message to your project. The message can be text, audio, or video. This one will take you to a recording of *Chasing Sunlight*, performed by Don Watts and Bob Melendrez.

DKBRJZTYQQ

Technique

The technique I used to insert the small Nine Patches into the border is fun and easy. First I made a long border of my two fabrics, one fused on top of the other and buttonhole stitched. It didn't need to be as long as the quilt top measured as I was going to insert 3" wide pieces into it.

This is my top border before any Nine Patches were inserted. I made the black-and-white Nine Patches, then added a piece of border fabric to two sides.

I auditioned the location and angle of a Nine Patch unit on the wall, then removed the border piece for cutting.

I trimmed off the excess fabric at the top and bottom, then sliced the border at the correct point.

I repeated that process for the length of the border although the four Nine Patch blocks in the corners of the quilt were fused and buttonhole stitched instead of inserted.

The National Quilt Museum
Expanding the Vision, Advancing the Art

The National Quilt Museum strives to bring the work of today's quilters to new and expanding audiences worldwide. It promotes the quilting community through exhibition, education, and advocacy efforts.

Exhibits

Museum in-facility and touring exhibits are annually viewed by over 110,000 quilters and art enthusiasts. In an average year, visitors come to the museum from all 50 states and over 40 countries to experience the art of today's quilters. Museum visitors experience over 13,000 square feet of extraordinary quilt and fiber art rotated 7-10 times per year. Both travelling exhibits and work from the museum's own collection are exhibited on a daily basis. The museum is a three-time TripAdvisor Certificate of Excellence winner.

The museum's touring exhibits can be seen at museums and galleries nationally and around the world. Recent travelling exhibits have been seen at Shafer Memorial Art Gallery, Great Bend, Kansas; Harlingen Arts and Heritage Museum, Harlingen, Texas; and the Branigan Cultural Center, Las Cruces, New Mexico.

Photo by Glenn Hall Photography

Education

Over 4,000 youth from kindergarten through high school annually participate in museum educational programs. Several of these programs have received national media attention. The School Block Challenge, sponsored by Moda Fabrics, is an annual contest in which participants are challenged to make a quilt block incorporating a packet of three fabrics. Now in its 24th year, this School Block Challenge continues to be utilized by schools and community organizations as part of their art curriculum in over 20 states. Over 500 students participated in the 2015 contest. Other popular youth programs include the annual Quilt Camp for Kids, Kidz Day in the Arts, and the Junior Quilters and Textile Artists Club.

Student with Judy Schwender, Curator of Collections. Photo by Glenn Hall Photography

Advocacy

As part of the museum's mission to bring quilting to new audiences worldwide, the staff works aggressively to spread the word about the extraordinary art created by today's quilt community. Last year alone, over 300 publications wrote articles about the museum's work including Reuters, Yahoo.com, and the International Business Times. In addition, in 2014 National Geographic magazine mentioned the museum as the anchor attraction making Paducah, Kentucky, one of the smartest tourist attractions in the world. Throughout the year museum staff members give talks and participate in panel discussions about the work of today's quilters.

If you are reading these words, you are most likely one of over 16 million active quilters from the United States and around the world. The National Quilt Museum is committed to supporting your work and advancing the art of quilting so that everyone worldwide can experience and appreciate your amazing work.

For more information about The National Quilt Museum, visit our website at www. NationalQuiltMuseum.org.

Gift shop manager Pamela Hill and volunteer Loyce Lovvo

The National Quilt Museum is a 501(c)(3) nonprofit organization funded by quilters like you.

More AQS books

This is only a small selection of the books available from the American Quilter's Society. AQS books are known worldwide for timely topics, clear writing, beautiful color photos, and accurate illustrations and patterns. The following books are available from your local bookseller, quilt shop, or public library.

#1547 . . . . $24.95

#8350 . . . . $26.95

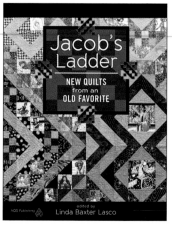

#1255 . . . . $26.95

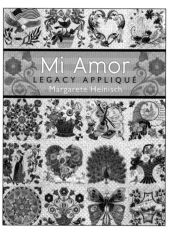

#1550 . . . . $24.95

#8152 . . . . $26.95

#8669 . . . . $26.95

#1251 . . . . $26.95

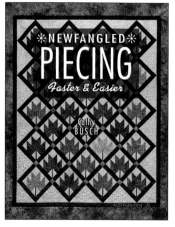

#1420 . . . . $24.95

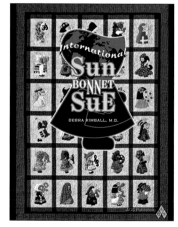

#8347 . . . . $24.95